The Complete
Book of Ferrets

Please renew/return this item by the last date shown.

So that your telephone call is charged at local rate,
please call the numbers as set out below:

	From Area codes 01923 or 0208:	From the rest of Herts:
Renewals:	01923 471373	01438 737373
Enquiries:	01923 471333	01438 737333
Minicom:	01923 471599	01438 737599

L32b

The Complete
Book of Ferrets

Val Porter and Nicholas Brown

D & M PUBLICATIONS

D & M Publications
PO Box 172
Bedford MK40 2ZJ

Published by the Penguin Group
27 Wrights Lane, London W8 5TZ, England
Viking Penguin Inc., 40 West 23rd Street, New York, New York 10010, USA
The Stephen Greene Press Inc., 15 Muzzey Street, Lexington, Massachusetts 02173, USA
Penguin Books Australia Ltd, Ringwood, Victoria, Australia
Penguin Books Canada Ltd, 2801, John Street, Markham, Ontario, Canada L3R 1B4
Penguin Books (NZ) Ltd, 182–90 Wairau Road, Auckland 10, New Zealand

Penguin Books Ltd, Registered Offices: Harmondsworth, Middlesex, England

First published 1985
Reprinted 1987
Paperback edition 1990
This edition 1997

Printed and bound in Great Britain by Butler & Tanner Ltd, Frome and London.

A CIP catalogue record for this book is available from the British Library.

ISBN 0–9522832–0–4

Contents

Acknowledgements

Our thanks are due to a large number of people who have generously and willingly given us so much of their time, expertise and knowledge. In particular we are grateful to the following:

BBC Natural History Unit
Sir George Bellew, KCB, KCVO
British Veterinary Association
Tony Buckwell, MRCVS
Maurice Burton
J.D. Burtoo
Tina Clayton
John E. Cooper, MRCVS, FIBiol, Royal College of Surgeons
J.M. Evans, MRCVS
Paul Flecknell, MAVetMB, PhD, MRCVS
David Garrod
Dr John Hammond, Jr
Percy Heath
R. Heathcote, MRCVS
Sheryl Hennessy, Editor, *Surveillance* (NZ)
Dr Jane Houghton
Mrs Elizabeth C. Howard, MRCVS
Colin and Jenny Hughes
Mike Jasper, Surrey Ferret Welfare Society
Col A.G.H. Jukes
John A. Knight, MRCVS, Zoological Society of London
Dr W. Mansi

Marilyn Marchant, PDSA
Marshal Gilman Research Animals Inc, New York
Alec Martin, National Ferret Welfare Society
Nick Mills, MRCVS
MAFF ADAS Ferret Mortality Project
Alan Mowlem, FIAT, MIBiol, National Institute for Research into Dairying
Roger A. Mugford, BSc, PhD
Michael Oxenham, BVetMed, MRCVS
Dr Trevor B. Poole, DSc
John Rainbird
Michael Rosenberg, Partridge Films
Sheffield University
Jackie Spencer
Tim Thomas, RSPCA
Universities Federation for Animal Welfare
Dr Alan Walker, BSc, PhD, FIFST, FRSC, MIBiol
Laurie Webb
Dominic Wells, MRCVS
Trevor Wise

Photographic Credits
Photographs are by courtesy of the following:

The British Library: p. 8 – from Queen Mary's Psalter (ref. Royal 2BVII folio 155v)

The Burrell Collection – Glasgow Museums & Art Galleries: p. 9 – The Ferreters tapestry (reg. no. 46/56)

The Courtauld Institute of Art; reproduced by kind permission of the Marquess of Salisbury, Hatfield House: p. 11 – The ermine portrait of Queen Elizabeth I

Nicholas Brown: pp. 12, 16, 19, 29, 32, 48, 49, 54, 110, 116, 118, 121, 128, 130, 131, 135, 136, 139, 145

Shaun Clarkson: pp. 19, 67

Mike Jasper: pp. 19, 42, 95, 96, 99, 101, 105, 107

Alec Martin: pp. 42, 60, 64, 67, 85, 115

Trevor Poole: pp. 16, 17, 38

Jackie Spencer: pp. 21, 33, 54, 79, 95, 96, 146, 148, 149, 152

Introduction

There is something about ferrets. Some people find them good working partners for a frosty morning's rabbiting. Some enjoy their individuality and admire their courage, or appreciate their affable companionship. Some react with a knowing laugh or a shudder. The majority, perhaps, dismiss ferrets as smelly animals that bite and that spend much of their time down the trousers of foolhardy men.

The majority are very wrong indeed.

This book is concerned first and foremost with the welfare of the ferret. It sets out to do away with the myths and misconceptions that have given the animal its undeservedly bad reputation. It is not the fault of the ferret, but of generations of a minority of ferret keepers who have either mis-understood the real needs and nature of the animal and have treated it callously, indifferently or just plain misguidedly, or who have sought to project an image of the fierce and vicious ferret – perhaps because they believe that such a creature reflects their own image of themselves. The 'virile' man affects to be dismissive of the 'treacherous' dogs and ferrets he claims to control; if his animals are not as unpleasant as he claims, if in fact they are innately friendly, then who needs Hector?

Fortunately, most people who keep ferrets, for whatever purpose, re-spect their animals and have a sound relationship with them.

In writing a book on ferrets, we have taken on a considerable task. We are fighting prejudices, and in fact more of those prejudices come from the minority who have kept ferrets than from the majority who have not. The ferret has served mankind well for centuries: it deserves better than preju-dice. But ferreters, veterinary surgeons, pet owners, laboratory workers, fur breeders, naturalists, students of animal behaviour and writers all have their own strongly held opinions about ferrets. As often as not they will disagree with everyone else, secure in the belief that they, from personal experience, know best.

We have therefore made a point of talking to a large number of people across a broad spectrum. All that these very different people have in com-mon is an interest in ferrets – whether that interest is academic, practical or passionate – and all of them are the most friendly and generous people you could meet, happy to spend hours on end talking about ferrets and happy to share their knowledge and observations. Once you get involved in ferrets you meet some lovely people! But that does not stop some of them being wrong about ferrets some of the time. We hope that this book will give them fresh insights into a subject they thought they knew well.

Sometimes old ferreters' tales prove to be sound, but sometimes their advice has become distorted with time and people continue to believe in the distortion. It is important to pause and to look more closely at why you do certain things. Is it perhaps because 'it's always been done that way'? That is not necessarily adequate justification, and it might possibly be prejudice.

It is essential to try to understand any animal for which, by virtue of 'ownership', you have become fully responsible. That animal is entirely dependent on you and the responsibility is a serious one, however little you might have paid for the privilege of 'ownership'. To understand an animal, think of it in the context of a social group. In any society – whether a village, a bat colony, a farmstead, a beehive or a pack of wolves – there are tacit rules which ensure that, on the whole, there is acceptance of one another and the society can remain intact and balanced, and can thrive. So we have looked quite closely at the behaviour of ferrets and also of polecats in the wild. If you understand *why* an animal behaves in certain ways – quite often because of the mutual constraints of its society or of its environment – you can learn how to encourage the animal to thrive under your care. That will be in the animal's interest which, as you have volunteered to accept responsibility for its wellbeing, should be your first priority. And if you hope to get any sort of a return from any animal – as livestock, as an aid to hunting, as a worker, as a companion – the benefits you receive will be far greater if you have the animal's welfare at heart and if you understand what you are doing.

Every aspect of keeping and caring for ferrets is included in this book. We have written it for the ordinary ferret keeper (a word used in preference to 'owner' – who can 'own' a living creature?). We have also written it for your local veterinary surgeon, because not all vets are familiar with ferrets. The veterinary section in Part II has been written in close cooperation with veterinary experts who have considerable experience with ferrets. The whole book has been written in consultation with ferreters, ferret clubs, animal welfare organizations, pharmaceutical companies, research laboratories and other experts of all kinds, to whom we are most grateful for their sound advice and generous assistance.

You may confess that you know nothing at all about ferrets and are eager to find out what you can, or you may believe you know it all already and will disagree on principle with what you read in this book. The old cliché is very true: the more you know, the more you realize just how little you really do know. We hope that *The Complete Book of Ferrets* will give you a genuine understanding of this spunky, playful and rewarding animal which has so much to offer the caring ferret keeper.

PART I

Polecats and Ferrets ✳ The Merits of Ferrets ✳ Handling
Accommodation ✳ Feeding ✳ Maintenance and Health
Breeding and Litters ✳ Working Ferrets ✳ Bag and Pot
Pets and Characters

1   Polecats and Ferrets

It may come as a surprise to a few ferreters and to a lot of music-hall audiences to learn that ferrets are by nature friendly, brave, talkative, indefatigably curious and playful, and quite prepared to accept human beings as equals. They don't fawn like some dogs; they are not as aloof as some cats; they are not as obedient as some horses; nor as contemplative as some cattle. They are independent, amiable and highly individual characters.

Acceptance and lack of fear of Man show that the ferret is a domesticated animal: it is of a species that Man has tamed and brought under his control so that he can make use of it. Domestication over a long period allows Man to adapt a species to perform a function that is useful to him, and controlled breeding of the species gradually leads to differences between the domestic animal and its wild ancestors. The characteristics that Man finds most useful in the animal are naturally encouraged.

Like any other creature, Man exploits sources of food, and one function of domestication is to control other creatures which compete with him for his food. Taking it a step further, it is to Man's advantage not just to control a competitor (by destroying 'vermin', for example) but also to make positive use of one animal's predatory instincts against another animal that Man considers to be a competitor. So he domesticated, for instance, the cat to get rid of rodents. With the ferret he went one stage further: first of all, perhaps, he domesticated the ferret to get rid of the rats that ate his food, and then he found more sophisticated ways of using the ferret by exploiting its natural instincts as an underground hunter and the natural fear of the hunted. He began to use the ferret to chase animals out of the safety of their burrows rather than simply to kill them. Once the victims were above ground, man had the opportunity of harvesting them. So the ferret, like the dog, served a productive function as well as being a pest controller.

As a sideline the ferret has a reasonably acceptable fur (known as fitch), and it can be an excellent companion to its keeper, but it is the harvesting of rabbits for which the ferret has largely been bred over the centuries and it is this role which has determined the characteristics of the species we know today. The fate of the ferret has long been connected with rabbits.

Domestication of the ferret goes back many centuries, possibly as far back as the fourth century BC when ferrets might even have been used to put down snakes. However, this is more likely to have been the mongoose, which looks not unlike a ferret but is a member of the civet family, a genus known as *viverra*. There is philological confusion here: the word 'viverrine' means 'of or like the ferret or the civet family' and in the past the Latin word *viverra* has been interpreted as 'ferret', so that the two species are easily confused. Ancient history and philology are minefields best left to the specialists, but there are plenty of other minefields to be explored when you start talking about the emotive subject of ferrets!

For example, what was the domesticated ferret's wild ancestor? It was the polecat. Even that simple statement will make some people as convulsed as a bag of ferrets! Which polecat? Was it the European or the Asiatic, the Siberian or the Ethiopian? Polecats are found in many parts of the world – they range throughout northern Europe and Asia and seem to be different subspecies in different areas. Even as locally as, say, Sutherland or Yorkshire, it is claimed that separate subspecies existed. Most people now believe that the ferret is simply a domesticated European polecat – or perhaps a domesticated Asian polecat, or perhaps ...! Research continues, very actively at present, and the European polecat seems to be the favourite: Clifford Owen's chapter on ferrets in *Evolution of Domesticated Animals* is well worth reading on the subject.

For the purposes of this book the ferret is a domesticated polecat. Ferrets and wild polecats successfully interbreed and each has the blood of the other somewhere in its parentage, because ferrets escape (often) and become feral, and because wild polecats have been introduced specifically to improve bloodlines in domestic stock. They have been mixing their genes merrily to a certain extent all through the long ages of ferret domestication, and it is in fact important for the future of the ferret that the wild polecat should not become extinct. For any domestic species, a continuing wild stock ensures that overselective breeding and lack of variety in the domestic animal can be rectified: there is always a pool of genetic variation which can be tapped to 'improve' the domestic species.

Fifty years ago arguments about whether ferrets and polecats were the same species featured regularly in country sports publications like *The Field*. Thirty years ago *Country Life* published an article by John L. Jones, 'Polecat or Ferret', about the capture in Gloucestershire of what was claimed to be a monster polecat, twenty-four inches from nose to tip of tail. It had been caught in a gin trap at Tytherington, about ten miles from Bristol, and the author, convinced that the only 'wild polecats' in Gloucester were in fact feral ferrets, went to some lengths to establish that it was indeed a 'polecat-ferret'.

Or was it? A local gamekeeper said firmly that the difference between polecats and ferrets was in the strength of the skull: the lightest tap would knock off a ferret, but a polecat was a tough nut to crack, so to speak. The author explored many intriguing trails and lines of thought in his article and finally consulted the Natural History Museum in London who somewhat deflated all the academic discussions about skulls, crossbreeding with North African polecats, secret incursions across the Sharpness bridge by Welsh polecats and so on, by stating categorically that the specimen's mask identified it as 'a polecat-ferret, that is, a domesticated variety of ferret, not a cross between a white ferret and a wild polecat. The polecat-ferret is the form of ferret which most closely resembles the wild polecat, but is always distinguishable from it by the much whiter face of the former. Wild polecats only have a little white on the lips and again just above the eyes: the rest of the mask is black.' Mr Jones was left wondering whether age might not whiten the polecat's mask. . . .

So it goes on. Discussions about possible differences in skull structure will no doubt continue at an academic level. It is an intriguing subject (is there a genetic difference between polecats and ferrets, or is it something to do with too many centuries of bread and milk?) but one that makes little difference to the ferret keeper, who is more interested in the everyday animal.

The desirable characteristics for which ferrets have traditionally been bred include tameness (in the sense of having no fear of Man), the instinct and ability to hunt and, for practical reasons, the white or creamy coat which most people automatically associate with 'pure' ferrets. The practical reason for favouring the light colour is that it is much more visible. There is also perhaps a slight mysticism associated with white animals, and there is even more mysticism associated with albinos, of any species. The 'true' or 'English' ferret is an albino, that is it lacks pigmentation so that not only is its fur white but also its eyes are pink. Those pink eyes identify it as an albino.

But a ferret does not have to be albino to be a ferret. It can be creamy, sandy, ginger, brown, almost orange in colour, or it can look remarkably like a wild polecat, with a dark brown coat over a cream or buff undercoat and with a characteristic mask. That mask gives a clue about where ferrets and polecats fit into the general pattern of species.

The Latin name of ferrets and polecats is *Mustela putorius*, with the occasional variation (the polecat has also been tagged *'foetidus'* and the ferret sometimes adds *furo* to its name). The *Mustela* prefix places them in the family *Mustelidae*, to which the majority of the carnivore species found in Britain belong. *Mus* is Latin for mouse but the ancients used it to include rats, martens, sables and ermines as well, and there is a theory that *mus* is derived from a Sanskrit verb *mush* meaning to steal. An etymologist might be able to say whether the term *Mustela* refers to a vague similarity

of general shape to that of mice, or a tendency to steal, or a shared fascin-
ation for holes, or, more likely, to the fact that the mustelids are predators
of mice. The Greek for a ferret, by the way, is based on the word for
rabbit, which is much more like its modern image!

Take a look at the family table below which shows you the ferret's
relations. You might be surprised that the badger is in the same family as
the ferret. It lacks the gracefully sinuous body of most of the other relations but it certainly shares some of the other common mustelid features
such as personal cleanliness, a faint musky odour, having five toes on each
foot (dogs, foxes and cats have four), living in holes in the ground (except
for the arboreal martens) and so on. The more active predators, like weasel,
stoat, marten, mink and polecat, nearly always eat the brain of their prey
first and you can therefore often recognize one of their kills, bitten through
at the base of the cranium. Note that the badgers include three species of
'ferret badger'!

Like other carnivores, the mustelids have anal scent glands (so does a
dog, for example) and in the mustelid these are particularly well developed.

The Ferret Family

CLASS: MAMMALIA
ORDER: CARNIVORA
FAMILY: MUSTELIDAE

SUB-FAMILIES:	*Mustelinae*	*Mephitinae*	*Lutrinae*	*Melinae and Mellivorinae*
	Weasels, polecats, mink, martens, grisons and wolverines	Skunks	Otters	Badgers and honey badgers

The Musteline Species

Mustela nivalis	– European common weasel	*Vormela peregusna*	– Marbled polecat
M. nivalis rixosa	– Least weasel	*Ictonyx striatus*	– Zorilla, or African polecat
M. erminea	– Stoat, or short-tailed weasel	*Poecilictis libyca*	– North African banded weasel
M. frenata	– Long-tailed weasel	*Poecilogale albinucha*	– African striped weasel
M. africana	– Tropical weasel	*Galictis vittata*	– Grison, or huron
M. felipei	– Colombian weasel	*G. cuja*	– Little grison
M. putorius putorius	– European polecat	*Lyncodon patagonicus*	– Patagonian weasel
M. putorius furo	– Ferret	*Martes martes*	– Pine marten
M. eversmanni	– Steppe polecat	*M. americana*	– America marten
M. nigripes	– Black-footed ferret	*M. melampus*	– Japanese marten
M. altaica	– Mountain weasel	*M. pennanti*	– Fisher, pekan, or Virginian polecat
M. sibirica	– Kolinsky, or Siberian weasel	*M. zibellina*	– Sable
M. kathiah	– Yellow-bellied weasel	*M. foina*	– Stone, beech or house marten
M. strigidorsa	– Back-striped weasel	*M. flavigula*	– Yellow-throated marten
M. nudipes	– Barefoot weasel	*M. gwatkinsi*	– Nilgiri
M. lutreolina	– Indonesian mountain weasel	*Gulo gulo gulo*	– European wolverine
M. vison	– American mink	*Gulo gulo luscus*	– North American wolverine
M. lutreola	– European mink		

They are controlled: they are used primarily to mark territories and, in solitary species, to lay a trail in the mating season. They might also be discharged at will, or instinctively, if the mustelid is alarmed or angry, and the biggest and boldest dog will back off from the smallest weasel once it lets off its stink glands. Droppings have a slightly musky odour. The polecat's glands are very well developed indeed: its musky discharge is proverbially potent, hence the *putorius* and *foetidus* tags. It is not quite as overpowering as its relative, the skunk, but the polecat has been called by several names referring to that potential smell: foulmart, foumart, fulimart are all versions of 'foul marten', for example. The well-kept ferret, however, does not 'stink like a polecat' – it has a mild pleasant everyday smell and will only discharge a stink under extreme provocation. Even then it is less potent than the polecat's, although the musk does tend to cling, particularly to wet clothes.

To return to the polecat's mask, as opposed to musk, you might like to compare the facial markings of polecats, badgers, skunks and pine martens. And pandas and raccoons ... We have not yet come across any convincing

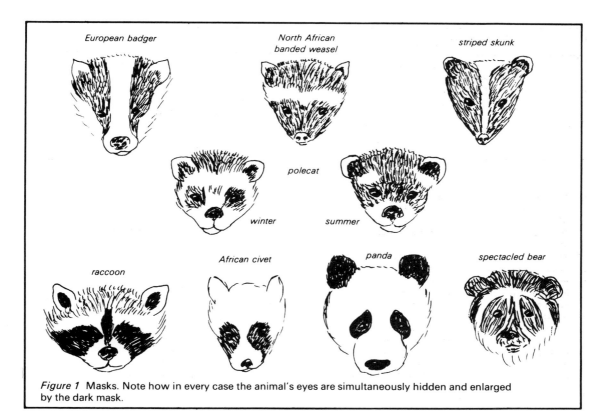

Figure 1 Masks. Note how in every case the animal's eyes are simultaneously hidden and enlarged by the dark mask.

theories about such masks but there is scope for speculation. Polecat-ferrets often have masks too, and the patterns sometimes differ between the same animal's winter and summer appearance.

Assuming the British polecats and ferrets are of European origin, ie *Mustela putorius*, which is found over most of mainland Europe (except Greece, Albania and Bulgaria), the wild species possibly came to Britain when there was a landbridge with the continent. The domesticated ferret, some say, came over to Britain with the Romans, although others say it was the Normans. It was probably closely linked with the introduction of the rabbit, which also has an uncertain history in these islands.

However, after the Norman conquest there are definite written and pictorial records of ferrets in Britain (and incidentally the first recorded rabbit colony was in 1176 on the Scilly Isles). The pictures are interesting. Take a look at the one below, which is a very early and fairly simplistic representation of two women putting a ferret to a netted rabbit bury. This picture comes from Queen Mary's Psalter and is dated about 1325 (the Psalter was actually presented to Queen Mary more than two centuries after it was originally produced). The manuscript is now in the British Library.

A more complex and interesting picture of ferreting is the fifteenth-century Franco-Burgundian tapestry (opposite) which shows peasants ferreting for rabbits. Look at the unconcerned rabbits! With all those people and all those dogs! And the dogs: there could be a lurcher in there, and there are some that look like miniature lions and bears which are probably a breed similar to the popular medieval English hunting dog, the Talbot, which is thought to be the ancestor of most of our scenting hounds.

Women ferreting. An illustration from *Queen Mary's Psalter*, c. 1325 (in the British Library).

Franco-Burgundian ferreting tapestry. 15th-century tapestry, now in the Burrell Collection, Glasgow. This tapestry is full of incident and character: men, women, dogs and ferret are all keen for the action.

Look, too, at the lines and nets (making due allowance for artistic licence). They probably *are* purse nets: the apparently rigid oval frame must in fact be a drawstring (look at the one being held in the bottom left-hand corner of the tapestry). And can you spot the ferret being taken from its basket (a good air-conditioned carrier, if a bit noisy for ferreting)? It is of course an albino, and a well-handled one too judging by the casual way the man is holding it.

In contrast to this stylized but practical scene, there is the sixteenth-century 'Ermine Portrait' of Queen Elizabeth I, now at Hatfield House. The queen is richly dressed and bejewelled, and on her left sleeve there is a small 'ermine' – a mustelid whose white fur is shown spotted with black and which wears a coronet around its neck. No such dappled creature ever existed; ermine is the winter coat of the stoat, which is white except for a black tip on the tail, and the familiar black-and-white pattern of lordly ermine trim is achieved by incorporating the black tail tips when the pelts are made up. So Queen Elizabeth's small pet is a mythical beast, and as ermine is a fur worn only by nobility it is probably meant to suggest that the Queen had the nobility well under her control. The animal's attitude is decidedly submissive. Many experts claim that the ermine represents virginity or purity, although one might think that all those black spots on it detract from that idea. Whatever it does represent, it seems unlikely that such a tame animal could be a stoat, even allowing for artistic licence, but it just could be that the Queen actually had a pet ferret, and a friendly, well-handled one at that.

'Well-handled' is a key phrase – it's basic to the philosophy of this book and to the real nature of the ferret. The animal is a natural killer, and it will kill for the sake of doing so as much as for a meal. That is why Man domesticated the polecat in the first place: he found ways of using its strong predatory instinct. A good ferret, however, is not employed to *kill* rabbits; it is used to bolt them from the safe inaccessibility of their buries so that a man and his net, or his gun, or his dog, can catch them.

Nor is a good ferret used to hunt people! He will not bite except with good reason. If you understand ferrets you will understand under what circumstances they might bite, and you will find that no real harm is intended unless the rules have been seriously infringed. Ferrets are not vicious.

Polecat and ferret names and associations have helped to perpetuate their falsely bad reputation. The polecat has also been known as fitche, fitchew and fitchet weasel, and the names are probably from the Dutch *visse* meaning nasty. (The fisher marten's name comes from the same root – it has nothing to do with fishing!) The word ferret comes from the Medieval Latin word *furo*, meaning furtive or thief-like. Go back a bit (forget that Norman invasion!) and the Anglo-Saxons had words for it too, but the same words seem to hold good for ferrets, weasels and martens – words based on *meard*, derived from the mid-Latin *martus*. One could go on.

Why 'polecat', then? One theory connects the name with the French words *poule* (chicken) and *chat* (cat), and it must be admitted that polecats (and ferrets) are very partial to a nice plump chicken at roost. This weakness is one reason why there are so few wild polecats in Britain today. A hundred years ago the polecat was common in England, Scotland and Wales but nineteenth-century gamekeeping was probably largely responsible for their virtual extinction by 1910 in England and Scotland, although there is still a thriving Welsh population. Polecats and many other predators have been persecuted by gamekeepers concerned for the safety of their reared birds, and the persecution has been both direct and indirect. A trap

The Ermine Portrait of Queen Elizabeth I by Nicholas Hilliard (1547–1619) (now at Hatfield House). The 'ermine' on the Queen's sleeve could be a pet ferret rather than a stoat.

set for a weasel or stoat is just as likely to catch a polecat, and several other things as well. The wild polecat retreated to a stronghold in Wales, although every now and then there are reports of other populations, like the Tytherington giants and the Yorkshire reds.

The polecat in the wild has been studied by several specialists over the last few years, notably Professor Trevor B. Poole, Nick Teall and Ken Walton, who have carried out long-term surveys into polecat distribution. Other people have studied them through the camera, like Heinz Sielmann (*Goblins of the Forest*) and Rodriguez de la Fuente (*The Secret Life of the Polecat*). Accumulated knowledge about the behaviour of polecats in the wild has been used throughout this book as a background to the ferret's natural instincts. This can, of course, be misleading: we have already suggested that domestication over a long period can cause an animal to alter its habits and its appearance – indeed if it failed to alter its habits it could not survive in captivity. But just as modern Man still harbours primaeval urges, however repressed or redirected, so must the ferret. In Man, the suppression of some of those urges and instincts might be harmful to him. So might it be for the ferret.

We'd like to say a brief word here about the ferret in the United States of America, where ferrets are increasingly popular as pets. There is a

Sleeping ferret

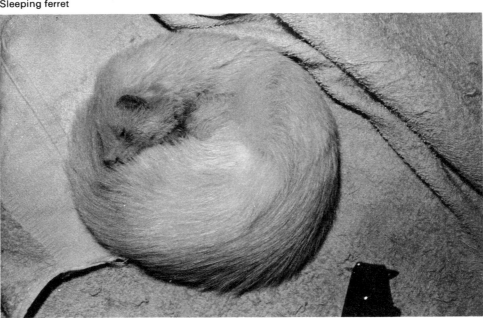

native North American animal, the black-footed ferret (*Mustela nigripes*), which is possibly descended from the South Siberian ferret and which once roamed wild on the Great Plains from Texas to Dakota. It used to live well on prairie dogs but since the latter were ousted by settlement and farming the black-footed ferret has become virtually extinct and very few specimens, if any, remain alive in the wild. But the ferrets familiar in Britain found their way to the United States via South America from Southern Europe, probably during the nineteenth century and probably as ratters on the ships that brought them. Ferreting became big business in America in the early 1900s, encouraged by the US Department of Agriculture, for the control of rodents and in due course for bolting rabbits, raccoons, gophers and a variety of other animals considered to be pests. But then chemicals took over in the war against rodents and ferreters found their livelihood disappearing. Some tried fitch farming but the tastes of fashion never turned to fitch. Today ferreting is not permitted in most states, but the ferret as a pet and as a laboratory research animal is alive and well and growing in numbers and popularity. The pink-eyed albino is commonly known as the English ferret in America.

In Britain, too, ferrets are increasingly popular as pets. Individual ferrets, some with fairly unlikely names, are described in Chapter 10 on Pets and Characters and should give you a good idea of why so many people find ferrets interesting and attractive. In the meantime, let's get down to some of the practicalities.

2 The Merits of Ferrets

Well, why do you want to keep a ferret? Here is an extract from a book published in 1902 called *Home Pets, Furred and Feathered*, by M.G.P. Fermor:

> The Ferret is not an attractive animal; quite the reverse. He is a member of the weasel family, and is supposed to be a native of Africa. It is, however, certain that he can only exist among us in a state of domestication. He is not to be trusted out of his cage without a muzzle, for instances have been known of sleeping children being attacked by ferrets who had entered a house unperceived. There are those who admit ferrets to the same terms of intimacy as cats, and will let the creatures crawl about them at will; but such folk must be deficient in the sense of smell, for, despite its personal cleanliness, this animal emits a strong, unsavoury odour.

If you have kept ferrets, no doubt you will react quite strongly to this extract! It epitomizes all those old prejudices about dangerous, stinking ferrets and it probably deprived a whole generation of readers of the pleasures of keeping ferrets. Print is powerful: it perpetuates myths. But at the same time the author of that piece does give one or two clues about the real nature of ferrets. They *are* expert escapers and are good at being 'unperceived'; they can be very friendly and affectionate, or they can be as standoffish as a cat; and they are clean by nature. On the other hand, most of his statements are very wrong indeed, and he has made the mistake of blaming the animal for its handlers. To rewrite the piece:

> The Ferret is an attractive animal. It is a member of the weasel family and is probably descended from the European polecat; it has been domesticated for several thousand years. It rarely needs to be muzzled, unless it has been badly handled in the past. Many people enjoy having their ferrets clambering over them, nestling in their pocket or down the front of their shirt, dozing in their arms or on their lap. Such folk are by no means deficient in the sense of smell; this animal is a very clean one and its odour is normally a light and quite pleasant musk, no more offensive than that of a dog or any other domesticated animal; it only emits a strong odour if very angry or alarmed.

Plenty of people do keep ferrets as house pets in Britain and they come from all walks of life. We have talked to policemen, shift workers, Lloyds brokers, writers, veterinary surgeons, miners, radio producers, sportsmen, carpet layers, secretaries, zoologists, television people, teachers, charity officials, lawyers, housewives, electricians, farmers, professors and quite a few youngsters who have pet ferrets. Sometimes they are simply pets; sometimes they also do a spot of work down a rabbit hole, to give them some exercise and interest and to give their keepers an excuse to be out and about in the countryside armed with a pair of binoculars and a camera.

Ferrets can make very good pets. They are endlessly entertaining, chatty, small and easy to look after. They do not need a great deal of space and hardly need any house-training. They do not have to be taken out for regular walks like a dog, although they take happily enough to a harness and lead. They are good pets for a responsible youngster who can learn a lot about ferrets and about caring for and respecting any animal, and also about the countryside if the ferret is used for rabbiting. Many a grown man has nostalgic memories of the pet ferret he used to carry with him everywhere when he was a boy, his constant companion whether out-of-doors or at home where his mother, more often than not, strongly disapproved of ferrets in the house. The joy of a ferret is that it is so portable and that it responds so well to a caring keeper.

Very young children, however, are not ideal companions for ferrets (nor, perhaps, for any other pets). They can unwittingly provoke an animal by failing to read the warning signs that say, 'You're pushing your luck – get off my back!' The subject of pets is considered further in Chapter 10.

You can keep ferrets for the occasional day's rabbiting or for more regular and serious sport (and we stress that it is sport – you won't make a fortune, or even a living, out of using ferrets for catching rabbits and rats). You can specialize in breeding ferrets for their fur or to supply laboratories, but these are competitive and professional areas and should only be tackled by people who know what they are doing. Fitch farming is growing very fast indeed in New Zealand and is practised commercially on quite a large scale, despite an old prejudice that fitch fur tends to fall out after a while and that it retains a lingering hint of the ferret's gentle musk. Mink, one should point out, has the same problem in respect of smell. Fitch farming is also practised in the United States and to a minor extent in Britain, where a few ferrets are sometimes kept on mink farms. Ferrets do have the advantage of being easy to handle, which mink never are, and also of being able to produce two litters a year and perhaps more under controlled lighting conditions. If you are considering professional fur farming we suggest you contact the Fur Breeders Association, but you will find that the market is already dominated by substantial and experienced breeders: there is no room for small-scale operators and very little welcome for newcomers. The same applies to breeding animals for research laboratories, which demand consistent and healthy stock.

A sideline to ferret keeping used to be the supply of fitch fur for 'Camel Hair Brushes' (Camel was the name of the owner of the brush business; the brushes were made from mustelid fur and not from camel's wool!) or for French *putois* brushes, traditionally made from polecat hairs and used for painting ceramic ware.

Young albino

Polecat in summer coat

You could also breed to supply other people with pets or workers but you will soon find that, in the season, there are an awful lot of surplus young ferrets around and unless yours are outstanding you may not find any market for them at all. However, it could be interesting to specialize in producing a particular colour or shape of ferret. Breeding has not been wholly scientific in the past and there is scope for careful, selective breeding, both for appearance and character.

Once you have decided why you want ferrets, what should your guidelines be for choosing your animals? Broadly speaking, you will be selecting for appearance, character, health and gender.

APPEARANCE

This heading includes the colour of the coat and the conformation of the body. Ferrets vary from pure albino to pure polecat, with a fair variety of coat colours and patterns in between. The pelt generally has a soft woolly underfur which is usually lighter in colour than the long coarse 'guard' hairs that give a sheen to the coat and diffuse the effect of the colouring.

The albino lacks pigmentation: its eyes are pink and its coat is often white but can have a creamy or even darker hue. This tinting is due to the activity of sebaceous glands, particularly in uncastrated males, who sometimes look almost orange. Sick albinos may also develop orange coats. Usually an albino is whitest in winter, turning light gold in summer.

Polekits. Polecat litters aged 3½ weeks and 7 weeks. All polekits have pure white fur at the age of one week. The kits on the left, whose eyes are still closed, are already developing darker coats. The older kits on the right are beginning to resemble adults and they will be fully grown at about three months old.

Albinism, as explained in Chapter 7 on breeding, is due to a recessive gene.

The pure polecat has a pale, creamy-buff undercoat. Its guard hairs are white at the base, shading to a yellowy-brown, with purple-black tips that are almost iridescent. In summer, after moulting during May and June in the northern hemisphere, the coat is much shorter and darker overall.

The facial markings of the polecat are striking. In summer the face is basically dark, with pale cheek patches and perhaps a few light hairs arching over the eyes. The fur on the ear tips is also very pale. These markings may change as the coat lengthens and thickens ready for winter: the ear tips remain pale but there is often a light band arching across the forehead above the eyes, over the cheeks and down to the jaw, so that the eyes are encircled by dark hair. Masks can vary considerably in the same animal at different times of year and at different ages. There may also be small white patches on the chin or the chest, but never as substantial as in a ferret. There is also a rare reddish European polecat.

The newborn polekit is pink-skinned with a sparse covering of white fur – just like any ferret kit. By a week old it is covered with pure white fur but two weeks later a new dark coat develops, with only the muzzle and ear-tips staying pale. By three months old it looks much like an adult but is slightly darker.

In between these two extremes of albino and polecat you can have all sorts:

A genuine *hybrid* between the wild polecat and a domesticated ferret looks very like a polecat. Its summer coat may give away its ferret parentage because it may have the typical winter polecat mask – with the band of white across the forehead from jaw-hinge to jaw-hinge rather than the eyebrow-and-cheek-patch style of the full-blooded summer polecat. The hybrid also gives itself away by its behaviour (see 'Character' below). It is often called a fitchet.

Polecat-ferrets are so called because of their appearance rather than their breeding. They are generally lighter in colour than the true first-cross hybrid, the guard hairs being dark brown rather than iridescent black, but they have similar facial markings. They are usually known as 'poleys'.

Sables have a dark brown coat over a buff undercoat, dark legs and tail and a dark mask across the eyes: not much different to a poley!

Sandies are all sorts, anything from a 'white' ferret with dark eyes (rather than the true albino's pink eyes) to a dark brown or almost black animal. They lack the polecat-type mask, and you might see, for example, a sable-coloured body, blond head and bib and pale feet.

Siamese have a very pale milk-chocolate look to the coat, and darker brown legs like a sealpoint Siamese cat.

Silver mitts are identified by their white feet (or mitts). They often have a white blaze on the throat or chest, and white streaks or patches on the head, back or tail tip. The basic colour is anything from very dark sable to a light tan, and they may have a dark mask.

Silvers are supposedly rare – they have been bred for a white undercoat with silver guard hairs mixed in with the usual dark or tan ones. Nothing to do with old age, you understand!

Moulting
Moulting is controlled by the ratio of daylight to darkness and can radically alter the appearance of a ferret. Winter and summer coats can be quite different, not only in density but also in colour and markings. There is an autumnal moult, followed by the growth of a thick winter coat with a good

ABOVE: Young 'poley'. The 'poley' or 'polecat-ferret' is not a first cross between a wild polecat and a ferret; it is a domesticated ferret with markings similar to those of a winter-coated polecat. Its guard hairs, however, are dark brown rather than the iridescent purplish-black of a true polecat.

BELOW: Ferrets come in a variety of shapes, colours and sizes and there is a considerable difference between their winter and summer looks: their coats are much thicker and their bodies much plumper in winter.

woolly underfur, during October/November in Britain. At the same time the animal piles on subcutaneous fat, and the winter animal is quite tubby, looking remarkably like a small bear. The pregnant female also tends to pile on fat, which she will need to draw upon when she is giving milk to her young.

The thick coat is usually thinned by partial shedding in early summer, when the wool and long guard hairs of winter are replaced by a much shorter trimmer summer coat. Winter fat is also lost and the slim summer ferret looks a shadow of its plump plush winter self. The female's moult usually occurs about three weeks after the first ovulation of the season, and as she is an induced ovulator (see Chapter 7) this means that an unmated female may not grow a short summer coat but will simply thin out the winter pelt by shedding. The mated female's moult may be gradual or may be quite dramatic and she can look almost bald in parts until she grows her new coat.

Spaying might result in a permanent change of facial markings and the female may lose her mask completely at the next moult. She might not grow such a thick winter coat in future.

All ferret kits start off white. It is just possible to tell albino from anything else while the eyelids are still sealed: you might be able to detect a slight dark patch through the eyelid of a non-albino. The undercoat and guard hairs take some time to develop and the final colouring will not be apparent until the kit is perhaps two or three months old. Even then it may change to some extent at the first moult. Nor does a kit have a mask at first, but if it is going to develop one it does so gradually, starting with small white patches below the ears.

Physique

Ferrets come in a range of sizes. Normally the females (called jills, bitches or does) are smaller than the males (hobs, dogs or bucks) and a really big hob next to a dainty poley jill can look as different as a bassett to a miniature dachshund. The basic *shape* is the same: a long slinky body (which tends to hump up in the middle when the ferret gallops or prances), quite short legs, a tail perhaps half as long as the body itself. But the total length of a full-grown ferret can be anything up to 24 ins (60 cm) or more, from tip of nose to tip of tail, and a hefty hob could have a winter weight of up to 5 lbs (2.3 kg), whereas a small jill might be only 15 ins (38 cm) long and weigh perhaps 1½ lbs (680 g) in summer.

There are several theories about why the male ferret is so much bigger than the female. It is quite a common feature in mustelids; for example in the European common weasel the female is half the weight of the male.

One theory is that the difference in size means that male and female avoid competing for food because they go for different prey, the male going for prey that is too big for the female to handle. Another theory is that male mustelids are promiscuous and territorial, and size is an advantage in laying claim to a territory or to a mate, whereas the female remains small enough to chase prey down burrows that are too tight a fit for the big male, and can also keep her litter down a hole that is inaccessible to the male.

The faces of some ferrets are fairly sharp, while others have a more rounded look to them. Face shape probably does not make much difference to anything: it depends on what you like. But in the past serious breeders of working ferrets have bred for a sharp muzzle, a long, supple and muscular body, and strong legs. A medium size was preferred for both ratting and rabbiting, although some chose smaller animals for ratting. Big ferrets were considered clumsy and slow but had their uses. It is a matter of personal choice: many people today prefer small jills for working. You cannot in truth say that the colour or size of a ferret is necessarily indicative of its character, which is the more important concern, except that it does seem to be true that a touch of true polecat tends to produce a livelier, smarter and shyer ferret.

A typically sharp-faced albino favoured by generations of ferreters.

CHARACTER

Character is a vital factor in choosing any animal and, like any other animal (including human beings), every ferret is an individual. You can no more say 'Ferrets are vicious' or 'Ferrets are good-natured' than you can say that all men are wise, brave or charitable. On the whole, ferrets are nice to know, but every now and then there's a born bad-tempered bully who is just plain awkward and who is unlikely to be trustworthy however well he is handled and cared for. Most so-called mean characters are only mean because of the way they have been treated. If you keep a dog on a short chain in the yard all day, never talk to it or handle it, and throw food to it when you remember to do so from a safe distance, you'll have a frustrated and bewildered dog which is more than likely to turn vicious. The same happens with a ferret kept in dark, filthy quarters and never spoken to or handled except when it is stuffed down a rabbit hole or a rat run. What sort of person would you be if you had comparable treatment?

We have already said that character is not necessarily associated with colour, although albinos tend to be a little more docile and polecats considerably more agile, alert, intelligent and independent. The albino has been selectively bred for centuries, and selective breeders have on the whole favoured the most manageable of their animals so that docility becomes bred into the stock. Quite often, however, someone would introduce wild polecat genes to liven up the bloodline.

It is unlikely that docility is actually inherent *because* the animal is albino, by the way; it is simply that albinos favoured for breeding have coincidentally been the tamer animals. It is possible that albinos of any animal are slightly 'weaker' in most respects – duller of wit and duller of senses – but that is a dangerous confusion of thinking. It is not necessarily the albinism itself that is responsible for the weakness. There may be some justification for thinking that albino ferrets have exceptionally weak eyes (the lack of pigmentation in the eye may render it more susceptible to disease and damage, and may also produce problems in vision, particularly in definition, but the logic is not proven any more than the theory that all white cats are deaf) but then *all* ferrets have poor sight in daylight. Think about the polecat's natural behaviour. It spends a fair amount of time underground, in darkness or semi-darkness, so that eyesight is the least important of its senses, although its night vision is in fact more than adequate for defining form and shape. You will find that most ferrets rely on their sense of smell, and hearing, and hardly bother to use their eyesight in daylight. Like many animals, especially those who spend some time underground or whose habits are nocturnal, ferrets are colour-blind: their world is in shades of grey. The polecat, incidentally, is a nocturnal or twilight animal, but the ferret, being domesticated, has learned to adapt to the habits of Man and has become an expert cat-napper at any time of the day or night – just one of several ways in which ferrets behave like cats.

Poor eyesight accounts for several aspects of ferret behaviour. They do not like jumping down from even a low height and that could well be because they really cannot judge where they are going to land. Distance to the ground is difficult to judge if you depend largely on your sense of smell! Some are not very happy climbers either, perhaps for the same reason: what goes up. . . . Poor eyesight also accounts for a lot of nips. A ferret's immediate reaction to something that moves suddenly is to taste it just in case it is food – make a quick grab at that blurred object because it could be a mouse, or a rabbit, or a worm. The surest way of having your finger bitten is to move it hesitantly towards a ferret and then jerk it away, as many children do. Hesitant movements are a very good imitation of a nervous victim. Ferrets are carnivores, remember.

A first-cross hybrid between the wild polecat and the ferret is much livelier than a ferret, much quicker, more eager to be off and away at the slightest opportunity, and less reliable in its relationship with its keeper. The young, if they remain with their mother (even if she is a quiet and friendly ferret), are nervous of humans, and in order to tame them at all it is necessary to separate them from the jill within two or three days of their eyes opening. Hybrids also seem to require a richer diet than does a common or garden ferret.

The breeding cycle can affect ferret character temporarily. Hobs are naturally more aggressive when they are in season (any time from early spring to mid-summer). They may very well look upon a man as a competitive male and have been known to think possessively of a familiar woman. In both cases rough treatment may be forthcoming, and the web between your thumb and first finger or the back of your wrist seem particularly to invite attention, whether aggressively against a man or roughly with a woman. At other times of year some hobs seem to be more docile than jills but that is a very broad generalization. However, a jill with a litter is bound to be less than friendly because she has young to protect: she won't even tolerate her mate for the first few weeks after the birth.

Ferrets on the whole are friendly, intelligent, spunky, industrious, conversational, endlessly curious and playful, and have many other equally attractive attributes, as you will find out for yourself.

HEALTH

The subject of health, or illness, is covered in depth in later chapters. When you are choosing a ferret it should, like any other animal, have a good coat with a gleam to it, not staring or ill-kempt (but don't forget what happens in the moulting season, when any ferret can look scruffy). The nose should be cool and slightly damp but not running or snuffly. The eyes should be bright and bold, and a properly handled animal will look you in the eye if nothing else distracts it (ferrets are endlessly inquisitive). Its general attitude should be alert and frisky, although ferrets like a good snooze at any time and can take quite a bit of rousing so that even the best might look dozy, especially in hot weather when any sensible ferret's urge is to find a cool shady spot for a siesta.

GENDER AND NUMBERS

Should you have hobs, jills or a combination? It is unfair on any species to keep just one; however attached an animal becomes to its owner, it needs its own kind as well. If you are concerned that this will make it less attached to you, then you are being downright selfish. Once you have watched ferrets enjoying each other's company, you will realize how important that company can be. For example, we heard recently of a sick jill which was normally kept with several others. It gradually became clear that she was dying, probably from bone marrow deficiency. The other ferrets seemed to be aware of this and they paid her special attention, behaving with great tenderness, grooming her gently and keeping her company quietly. In more cheerful circumstances they are usually a sociable lot. They often bicker but rarely fight seriously, unless two whole males are together in the breeding season and there is no escape route for the one that wants to back down.

The wild polecat is quite a solitary creature. Male and female have their own territories, possibly overlapping to some extent (though two males will never overlap). They pair up in the season for the serious business of propagating the species but even then they have separate quarters. A male's territory may accommodate several females in the breeding season. A pair will enjoy each other's company for a while – they will play like kittens – but there are limits to togetherness and the hob is no longer welcome once the litter is about to be born. The young family stays together for several months and the kits are in constant conversation: Rodriguez de la Fuente's film about Spanish polecats was memorable for the continuous chattering and playing. The hob was not part of this family scene, but the jill chattered endlessly to her litter, sometimes scolding, sometimes reassuring, sometimes gossiping.

From centuries of being housed together at close quarters, ferrets have regained the pleasure in each other's company which is still evident in a family of young polecats. So go for at least a pair of ferrets – a hob and a jill, or two jills, or even two hobs; but first of all think carefully about how much space you can provide for them. The breeding season can last for several spring and summer months each year and you will want extra accommodation if you need to separate your hob from the jill. A castrated hob or 'hobble' can sometimes be left with the jill but he will not be tolerated once her litter is due, and if she does have a litter you will need plenty of space for the fast-growing family. Litters average eight or nine kits, and there can be two litters a year.

Two in-season jills kept together and not mated or brought out of season by artificial means could get rough with each other and may need to be separated. A vasectomized hob will not give the jills a litter but he could still give them very sore necks if left with them for too long. And two hobs certainly need to be separated in the season, unless both have been castrated.

In terms of character, generalization is of course dangerous but some think that jills make better, spunkier and more intelligent workers, the theory being that as they have the natural role of feeding the young (hobs take no part in rearing the litter), females need to be better and more active hunters and killers of prey. Some people are prejudiced in other directions, wary of the potential problems of unmated jills. It is a matter of personal preference.

BACKGROUND AND SOURCES

An animal's background can be crucial to your choice, particularly if you are not experienced. Only buy from someone you can trust. Your possible sources are pet shops, country markets, gamekeepers, shows, ferret clubs, newspaper advertisements, veterinary surgeons, RSPCA and PDSA, or private breeders. Whoever you buy from, go to their premises, see how their animals are kept and watch them as they handle the animals to see how the animals react to them. There should be no fear or aggression on either side.

Join your local *ferret club* before you even think of getting your own ferrets. You can learn a great deal from other people's experiences, even if some of it is old ferreters' tales that should perhaps be taken with a hefty pinch of salt. Ferret clubs vary but most of them are concerned primarily with the welfare of the ferret rather than of its keeper. Membership might enable you to buy equipment at a cheaper rate, and sometimes gives you access to a vet at special club rates (if he treats six animals at the same time, it could be cheaper than a one-off). Some clubs pool their breeding hobs to keep bloodlines open. Some *may* be able to help you find a patch of rabbit land for ferreting but your membership will be much more appreciated if you ask, 'What's in it for the ferret?' rather than 'What's in it for me?'. Ferreting rights are hard to come by and must be earned, through whatever channels.

All clubs will share their knowledge and experience, usually over a few pints at the local. If you are sensible, you will be able to go out with experienced club ferreters so that you can see what it is all about before you get involved in buying your own ferrets or building hutches and acquiring gear. The National Ferret Welfare Society can give you the name of your local ferret club contact.

Gamekeepers are about the best contact you can have and it is well worth making yourself useful to a gamekeeper long before you get a ferret. If you prove yourself (and that will take some doing) you might be able to buy good ferrets off him and you might even be given permission to work the rabbits on his land. Tips on contacting gamekeepers, farmers and others who control rabbiting rights are given in Chapter 8.

If you are buying from a *pet shop*, be sure that the shop is a reputable one. However, this is probably the least likely and most expensive source of ferrets in this country – and price is not necessarily a reflection of quality. In the United States, where pet ferrets are much more popular, pet shops are a good source; they will supply a guarantee of health and they will ensure that the ferret has had its distemper vaccination. Whereas in Britain ferrets are sold for as little as £2 to £5 apiece, in the States the prices are much higher, anything from $20 to $80 each, and for a little bit more you can buy your ferret already vaccinated, castrated or spayed, or even pregnant and date-mated (at the maximum price). These higher prices are no bad thing for the ferrets: they ensure that ferret keepers take their responsibility to the animal as seriously as they should. It is sad to report that in Britain the ferret has always been regarded as cheap and therefore dispensable, and while it may be an advantage to those who keep ferrets, it has meant generations of ignorance and misconception about the ferret's needs.

Private breeders are often anxious to get rid of excess young stock around late summer. They may advertise in the local press or on noticeboards, or you may simply hear of them by word of mouth, particularly if you join a ferret club. It is important to visit the private breeder's premises and see what sort of conditions he offers his animals. Check on the parents (although you usually have no guarantee which is the father!) because parental traits, especially if they are strong ones, will probably be passed on to the young. Find out if the kits have been handled regularly from an early age and watch the breeder as he handles his animals. If he seems to expect to be bitten, he has not done a good job of rearing. No one wants a ferret that bites, but some people are their own worst enemies: they do not really understand their animals and they do not give them enough time every day. No ferret keeper should neglect playing with his animals, however trivial it might seem: it is through play that good relationships can be formed. Talking to them is just as important.

AGE

Ideally you should acquire a new ferret when it is 8–10 weeks old – old enough to leave the litter but young enough to learn quickly, especially if its breeder has been handling it from about half that age. Most litters are weaned at around 6–8 weeks old.

PURPOSE

So how do all these characteristics and criteria affect your choice of ferrets for particular purposes? For the sake of simplicity, let's reduce the categories to rabbiter, ratter, racer, pet, pelt and lab. Everyone has their own idea of the perfect type of ferret for each category – the diversity of ferrets is one of their attractions – and we can only give some broad outlines for beginners. You will soon find out which type of animal is right for you.

Rabbiters

Chapter 8 describes in some detail the qualities you will look for in rabbiting ferrets. First of all, bear in mind that ferreting for rabbits is not going to make you rich, although ferreted rabbits fetch a better price than shot ones. You will go ferreting for sport, for the pot, to exercise your ferrets or to help control an excess of rabbits. There was an experiment in New Zealand in 1884 when ferrets, weasels and stoats were deliberately introduced to try and control the rampant European rabbit population that was devastating sheep pastures. They did not succeed in keeping down the rabbits, although the ferrets themselves did well and established sizeable feral colonies. However, in later years ferrets and feral cats were given the run of a 21-acre enclosure on a New Zealand farm and between them they virtually eliminated the rabbit population over three years. The original population had been as dense as 48 rabbits to the acre. There are far more efficient methods of exterminating rabbits than with ferrets, but ferrets used with purse nets do give you 'clean' rabbits for the table or for your butcher.

The most important quality in a rabbiting ferret is that it should persuade the rabbit to leave the safety of the burrow. You do not want the ferret to *kill* rabbits. Contrary to old beliefs, however, there is no need at all to muzzle the ferret to prevent it killing, nor should it be starved before a day's work in order to encourage it to do its job. Most ferrets hunt for the sake of it: it comes naturally to them, however well fed they are, as it does to cats. They enjoy exploring the buries, and the rabbits would rather bolt out of the way than face a ferret. The right ferret for the job rarely catches a rabbit and it does not need to be muzzled or to suffer any of the appalling preventive measures of the bad old days such as having its teeth snapped off, its lips sewn together, or its jaws ringed.

The physiology of the albino eye, incidentally, is such that its accuracy of sight is particularly poor, which must make hunting a slightly haphazard occupation, however good the sense of smell. That might be one of the many reasons why albino workers have been favoured over the centuries of domestication: an albino might be less than adept at actually catching a rabbit but just as useful at scaring it out of the bury, which will be to the advantage of the ferreter.

Ratters
Use a ferret for ratting if you must but be aware that the ferret could receive a mauling: rats will not want to stand up to a ferret but a cornered rat may have no option. You need a fast, strong and exceptionally brave animal for ratting. All ferrets are brave but facing a cornered rat is asking a lot of even the fiercest hunter. More about ratting in Chapter 8.

Racers
Ferret racing is an increasingly popular sport at shows and pubs. It is a simple set-up: ferrets are put in at one end of long pipes and bets are laid on which ferret comes out the other end first. They have to come right out of the pipe. Most ferrets are only too happy to explore these artificial buries and they tease the punters by poking out an enquiring nose at the exit and promptly withdrawing again for further investigation. Ferret racing is a light-hearted sport – long may it remain so – and as so much is down to chance and inclination we can give you no guidelines on your choice of animal! The racing will anyway be incidental to whatever other lifestyle you want for your ferret.

Pets
Chapter 10 tells you more about pets. The choice is very wide and depends entirely on personal likes and dislikes. Character, of course, is important, and early and regular handling is a great character-former, both for the ferret and for its keeper. Pet owners must remember to respect their animals and to be prepared to change their own habits and attitudes in the interests of their pet rather than forcing the pet to change its nature.

Racer contemplating the finishing line.

Pelts

'Fitch' is the name for ferret or polecat pelts. If you want to go in for fitch farming you will have to do so on a large scale and you will have to know what you are doing. It is a complicated subject, where breeding and management are vital to success, and you would be well advised to talk to the Fur Breeders Association. Fitch farming is popular in New Zealand and you will find the New Zealand Ministry of Agriculture helpful. In this country the Min of Ag is more familiar with mink than fitch farming but will be able to put you on the right tracks. There is plenty of scope for breeding new colours and for improving pelt quality.

Labs

Research laboratories use ferrets for a variety of reasons. Their staff are getting over their prejudices: it used to be the case that they preferred handling cats or hamsters because they expected to be bitten by ferrets (have you ever examined a hamster's teeth?) but the lab ferret is a very docile and manageable animal, despite (or perhaps because of) the soul-destroying conditions in which it is often kept. The Universities Federation for Animal Welfare (UFAW) sets down guidelines about the welfare of lab ferrets to make their lives more tolerable.

Ferrets have been used extensively for research into human influenza (ferrets readily catch your colds or 'flu) and into vaccination against distemper (they are highly susceptible to canine distemper). They have been kept in large numbers for investigations into all sorts of diseases and defects, and into the phenomenon of photoperiodicity, ie the way in which the length of daylight or darkness affects breeding cycles (see Chapter 7).

If your conscience allows you to breed for supplying laboratories, you must be efficient and professional in your approach. The labs want consistent and healthy stock and often prefer to breed up their own colonies rather than risk bringing in infection or unwanted traits by purchasing from breeders. However, there are a few large-scale breeders who do supply labs and it is most unlikely that you will be able to break into that market.

Other uses

The ferret's insatiable desire to investigate dark holes and burrows has been used to good effect in a variety of ways. Ferrets can find jobs in any industries that use pipes. They have been employed to feed cables through underground conduits or to help clean out all manner of tubes and pipes: a piece of string harnessed to the ferret at one end and the smell of a rabbit at the other, and the ferret happily draws the string along the length of the pipe so that the cable or cleaning gear can be drawn through after it.

★   ★   ★

Whatever your choice, whatever your fancy, make sure that you are ready for your ferret before you fetch it in. Read this book from cover to cover beforehand; build a good, escape-proof home and exercise run; check out where your regular food sources are; warn your vet; join your local ferret club; and establish good relations with landowners and gamekeepers if you want to go ferreting. Never buy on impulse and bring a ferret home in your pocket from the Game Fair when you have no home for it. Ferrets are cheap to buy and cheap to keep, but price is no criterion of worth. They are living creatures who are entirely dependent on you. The dependence of one animal on another is a serious responsibility.

3 Handling

Let us destroy a myth once and for all: most ferrets do *not* bite. The occasional exception has either been badly or infrequently handled, or you have misread the basic rules of social behaviour. Only very rarely is the ferret a born biter.

Handling a ferret regularly and kindly is just as important as providing it with clean living quarters and the right food. An unhandled ferret is an unmanageable ferret, and that is not desirable whether it is a pet, a worker or anything else. Manageability is part of good ferret management and makes life simpler and more pleasant for the handler and for the ferret. Handling makes for trust, which is the essential basis of any relationship.

The basic rules for handling are:

1 Be positive, confident, calm and friendly in your approach.
2 Know what you are doing.
3 Keep all your movements smooth and decisive.
4 Use your voice as well as your hands – the sound of you should be as familiar as the smell and touch of you.
5 Start handling young ferrets as early as possible, preferably before their eyes are open, and thereafter handle your animals as often and as much as possible.

We have already mentioned that a ferret's eyesight is its least well developed sense. Also it is an expert predator and its reactions to anything that moves must be reflex and instant. A hunting polecat can strike its prey within one-twelfth of a second and such fast reactions can be triggered off by the slightest movement, or by prominence. A human finger or nose could be mistaken for prey in the heat of the moment, especially if it is hesitant and backs away again. So be direct in your approach and pick up the ferret in one smooth motion. Use your voice before and during the movement: mice and rabbits do not sound like humans and if the ferret is used to humans it will respond to your voice. It is anyway advisable to encourage a ferret to come willingly to your call (which it will do if, like a cat, it is in the mood) rather than to grab at it without warning. The aim is that the ferret should be happy to be handled and that it should not associate handling with unpleasant experiences.

PICKING UP AND HOLDING A FERRET

A ferret that is used to being handled can be picked up quite casually with a gentle hand under its chest, as if it was a small cat. Let the ferret know what you are up to: talk to it, stroke it and let it see you before you reach for it. An alternative hold is to spread your hand over its shoulders: if you are sure of a good reception hold it with your thumb and forefinger over one shoulder, the back of the neck in the fork between your first and second fingers and your other fingers over the second shoulder, or you can slide your hand over from the front instead of from behind. Most ferrets fit comfortably into your hand like this.

If you have doubts about the ferret's reactions to restriction, hold it firmly but kindly with your thumb and forefinger encircling its neck so that it cannot bite your hand. As with most animals, it is essential that the ferret respects you and knows what your tolerance threshold is. The direct approach and firm hold from above makes it clear who is in control. Don't let a young ferret bluff you, but also give a reward when it is due. Ferrets respond to affection and respect; they will invite you to pick them up and give them a good chest rub, and they will express their satisfaction by chuckling, sometimes hysterically. Pet ferrets enjoy curling up in a pocket or taking a snooze on a lap or along an arm.

They are, however, active animals most of the time and will probably wriggle in your grip but there is no need to squeeze tightly and indeed if you do so it will be unpleasant for the ferret and it will not be so happy to be picked up next time. Most ferrets are quite content to dangle from the holds we have described, but if the animal is pregnant or overweight you should also support its hindquarters with your other hand.

A well-handled ferret can be held comfortably around its shoulders. If you are not familiar with the animal, hold it firmly (but kindly) with your thumb and finger around its neck but without squeezing or pinching. All your handling movements should be calm, smooth and deliberate.

Never suspend a ferret by its tail. Not only is it unpleasant and undignified for the ferret, but also any offended ferret worth its salt can twist around and bite you from such a position.

The holds we have described will usually give such a feeling of security that the ferret yawns and relaxes. If it is restless, try the knuckle trick. Using both your hands, hold the ferret gently under its elbows and stroke its forepaw knuckles with your thumbs. Some ferrets find this irresistibly hypnotic and are lulled into a dream, their dangling bodies growing longer and longer as their eyes close. Every ferret has its favourite tickling spot and by handling your animal frequently you soon learn what it likes best – knuckles, chest, belly, behind the ears and so on.

Jills, like many other animals, carry their young by the scruff of the neck. However, if you try this on a mature animal you might trigger the wrong reaction. An adult ferret may well resent being treated like a juvenile and there are also more potent stimuli involved. The scruff, which is not very loose in the ferret, is a prime target for aggression and in making the jill receptive to mating, so your intentions might be mistaken. Think ferret!

The more you handle your ferret, the more amenable it will become. Make a point of handling it several times a day if time permits (and if time does not permit, should you keep an animal?) and not only when you clean out the hutch. It is best not to handle it while it is eating, and certainly

The knuckle trick: before and after. Most ferrets like to dangle from a comfortable hold around their shoulders or under their elbows. Stroking their knuckles can often induce complete relaxation.

not during mating. Encourage it to wander over your shoulders and along your arms; pass it from one hand to the other frequently; carry it around with you so that it learns to trust you completely. Get it used to your feet, too. If you start when the ferret is young, handling is simple. An older animal, or one that has been badly handled in the past, takes more patience but it is usually worth persisting.

INTRODUCTIONS

If you have just brought home a new ferret, put it in its own quarters and give it time to settle and find its bearings. Ferrets are methodical in their exploration of unfamiliar surroundings and will check out every boundary, on the alert for potential bolt-holes. Make sure it has access to a drink and leave it in peace. After a while, feed it and be alone with it while it eats. Talk to it quietly so that it begins to know your voice and your smell and learns to associate you with the good things of life, like food. Do not attempt to handle it until it has eaten. After a meal it will be comfortably sleepy and much more amenable.

When you are both feeling relaxed, offer the back of your tightly closed fist. A little milk on the fist will invite a lick rather than a nibble, and a little human spittle is even more attractive. Do not expect to be bitten, but do anticipate the possibility with an unknown and unsettled ferret, and only handle it when it is happy to be held. If it wriggles, let it go. You have plenty of time to get to know each other.

BITTEN?

A ferret that does bite may have already learned to associate fingers with a resented loss of liberty, especially if the previous handler has been rough or inclined to pinch and squeeze. With patience, even such a wary animal can be persuaded to accept that handling does not necessarily have unpleasant consequences.

A ferret that bites in earnest will hurt you. It can sometimes bite to the finger bone if it is provoked, but it will not cause as much damage with its puncturing teeth as will an angry rabbit with its powerful incisors which can just about take your finger off! And a cat bite is more likely to become infected than a ferret bite. So, if it is any consolation, even though the ferret bite hurts at the time and throbs like toothache later, you are not likely to die from it! The main problem is that a serious biter will not let go and the jaw is so designed that you will find it almost impossible to unlock its grip without actually breaking the ferret's jaw. There is a special pressure point somewhere just above the eyes where a deft thumb can work wonders, and a pinch on the foot could work as well.

The quickest release is by dunking the ferret's head in water, under a running tap or in a bucket. If you are in real trouble you can as a last resort press a finger against the animal's windpipe so that it has to let go to breathe, but by that stage it will probably have decided that you are an enemy and it will latch on again in a flash, in self-protection. Usually no drastic action is needed and quite often you will find that the only reason it *is* hanging on is because you have suspended it in mid-air and it does not know how far away the ground is. If you let it find its feet, it will probably let go in sheer relief at being down-to-earth again.

Except in very rare cases, ferrets are not out to get you. If you do get bitten, it is nearly always your own fault for not reading the social messages properly, for getting in the way when the ferret is excited about something (like rabbiting), or for acting as if you were prey or competition. Think ferret, and know your ferret.

Training a youngster means starting young. All young carnivores, including puppies and kittens, try out their milk teeth on anything that is available, including each other and humans. These nips are never serious, merely exploratory, and a young ferret is the same. When it is very young you can persuade it not to bite by pushing your finger knuckle into its mouth firmly a few times. With an older animal, force your clenched fist into its mouth, *make* it try and bite so that the experience is an unpleasant one for the ferret. Two or three sessions of this cures almost any ferret of biting. Remember to be equally generous with an affectionate stroke and tickle after the knuckle session, but never tolerate biting. A ferret must learn its limits.

We have not mentioned gloves for good reason. If gloves are to be effective against a ferret's teeth they must be thick and will probably be fairly stiff. You cannot handle any animal sensitively through thick stiff gloves, and from the animal's point of view such handling is bound to be uncomfortable and disturbing so that its fear and aggression increase. Only use gloves if the ferret is genuinely bad-tempered – and if he is there is probably little point in keeping him anyway. It is a complete fallacy to believe that the only good working ferrets are the evil ones. A good predator is efficient, not vicious, and a good working ferret *must* be easy to handle. Ferreting is an art, and there is no reason to make it more difficult than it already is!

ESCAPES

Ferrets always want to be somewhere else, their curiosity knows no bounds. They also seem to have little homing instinct and an escaped ferret – whether it escaped by intent or happened to find itself on the loose

– will go for a wander without any particular aim. It may find itself a comfortable home of its own choosing nearby (perhaps under a neighbour's shed or in a woodpile) or it may go far afield. Many a ferreter has had to leave his animal down a bury but usually retrieves it easily enough by leaving its familiar carrying box by the bury entrance.

It is tactful not to own up to an escaped ferret! They can cause considerable damage to, say, chickens. It is not that they are bloodthirsty; it is simply that all carnivores have to work hard for their food – most prey does not sit around waiting to be caught – and the predator must therefore always be ready to take advantage of a windfall because it never knows when it will catch the next meal. This very natural instinct to kill while you can has made ferrets, polecats, weasels, stoats, foxes and other carnivores unpopular with gamekeepers and poultry farmers to the point of victimization. Yet natural selection must favour a predator that makes the most of an unexpectedly easy catch where the prey does not or cannot escape, and it is nearly always through human intervention that such a situation can exist. An enclosure of chickens is an invitation to any carnivore, including ferrets. (An incidental piece of useless information: female turkeys will happily brood a stuffed polecat that contains a loudspeaker broadcasting the calls of young turkey chicks!)

Once a ferret has spent some time in the wild, it may be relieved at being found or it may resent it. Approach it with some caution and be patient. If you have the foresight, make a box for just such a situation and make sure that the ferret becomes familiar with the box in its daily routines and associates it with the good things of life, like food. Take the box with you when you are on the trail of the truant, and also take a length of pipe of some kind. It is more likely to dive into a promising pipe than into your grasp. Have its box ready at the other end of the pipe, with a food lure in the form of its favourite titbits, then just be patient. Once it has been recaptured, continue to be patient while it gets to know you again.

To return to the policy of disowning an escaped ferret, your best bet if someone asks you if you have lost one is to say no but to offer to catch the loose animal as you happen to know a little about ferrets. In that way you might be thanked rather than abused.

WARNING SIGNS

A wild polecat, which is normally a solitary animal, reacts characteristically to an intruder in its territory. Professor Trevor B. Poole has studied the behaviour pattern closely. In his description, the territory owner takes a sniff at the intruder's anal glands and then leaps on to its back to bite at its scruff. But this is only a gesture: the intruder ignores the insult unless

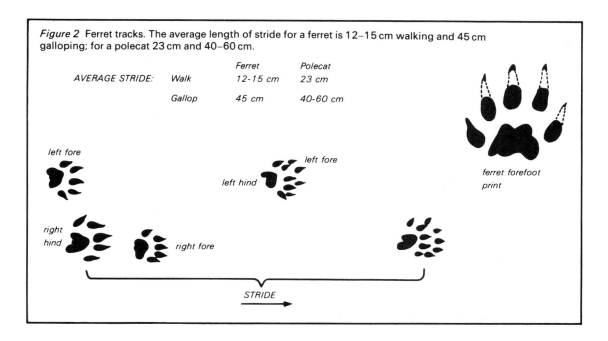

Figure 2 Ferret tracks. The average length of stride for a ferret is 12–15 cm walking and 45 cm galloping; for a polecat 23 cm and 40–60 cm.

		Ferret	Polecat
AVERAGE STRIDE:	Walk	12-15 cm	23 cm
	Gallop	45 cm	40-60 cm

left fore

left fore

left hind

ferret forefoot print

right hind

right fore

STRIDE

the owner persists, in which case the intruder will hiss and give a warning bite but will then continue to investigate the territory, sniffing at and sometimes overmarking the owner's scent-marked areas. All the while the owner follows, sniffing, biting at the intruder's scruff and dancing around it.

In due course the intruder satisfies its curiosity about the territory and turns its attention to the owner, first by sniffing at its anal glands and then by performing a characteristic dance. Facing each other, both animals jump into the air, twisting their bodies and opening and closing their mouths. The dance is repeated while they gradually move away from each other, until a safe distance is established and each can go its separate way, honour satisfied without any damage. But in the breeding season two males will be much more aggressive and will fight quite seriously, gripping each other by the scruff and shaking. Usually one or the other gives way and relinquishes the territory. During such a wrestling match, an intimidated animal which has no clear escape route will bare its teeth, arch its back, and hiss or scream at its opponent. This is a characteristic response to danger, and a very loud high-pitched scream is a sign of real fear, often accompanied by the release of musk from the anal scent glands.

Those scent glands are important in the social behaviour of carnivores. Their main purpose is to deliver complex messages about the sex, status,

Hissing polecat. This is a typical polecat attitude in reaction to a threat: it bares its teeth, raises its fur and hisses like a cat. If seriously alarmed it screams and releases a powerful musk from its anal glands.

age, reproductive condition and even diet of an animal. They have subsequently been adapted for territorial delineation, and in some of the mustelids – notably the weasel families (including the polecat) and the skunks – they have found an even more sophisticated role as defence weapons. The polecat's explosion of musk, sometimes deliberate and often involuntary in reaction to fear, combines with unmistakable warning behaviour, its striking facial pattern and coat-fluffing to produce a very effective defence against opponents or potential predators. Indeed the polecat has few predators other than Man.

Polecat youngsters play constantly with each other and in their play they seem to be preparing for the more serious encounters of adult life, learning the social rules. Young ferrets skitter about in much the same way: there is a lot of mock aggression, dancing, chattering, chasing and pouncing. One of them might pretend to protect a burrow entrance and the rest of the litter will make mock attacks, snapping and prancing at the presumptuous protector. Tag and wrestling are common activities, with a bit of biting at necks and ears. When an individual opts out of such games, it may do a quick dance before it retires to the nest or it may simply flop to the ground and lie limply. A limp attitude is also characteristic of a consenting female during mating.

This diversion into the behaviour of polecats and youngsters might give an insight into a ferret's likely reactions to certain situations. Like most animals, aggression towards another member of the same species is usually well orchestrated so that neither party suffers serious damage. Serious aggression is only likely if the rules are not observed or if no escape route is open to a potential loser. The main warning signs are the combination of arched back, fluffed-out tail, bared teeth and hissing. Very cat, and very ferret.

4 Accommodation

The wild polecat lives in an underground burrow, either appropriated from another animal or dug out for its own purposes using its sharp-clawed forefeet to loosen the soil and push it out between its hindlegs in a heap. An overhanging tree root or rock is a useful lintel.

The main burrow may have more than one entrance, so that there is always an alternative escape route or bolt-hole. Side chambers are scraped out along the close-fitting tunnel for a sleeping place and a larder, and the sleeping chamber is lined with dry nesting material which is piled up in some bulk for winter warmth. Much like its cousin the badger, the polecat keeps its nest scrupulously clean and sometimes drags out the bedding for a good airing.

Depending on the size of the territory, the animal may have several secondary burrows where it can take refuge in an emergency or take a kill for instant consumption or storage. Stored food is often forgotten and never cleared out, so that in the course of time it rots away.

The animal never defecates or urinates in or near its burrow. It tends to mark its above-ground territory with its droppings and backs up against a vertical surface, such as a rock or tree-stump, much like a dog choosing lamp-posts and thistles.

A nesting jill digs out a special chamber for her young, usually at the end of a run and well away from the entrance. She piles in plenty of bedding in preparation for the litter.

From these descriptions of the wild animal, you will realize that a ferret's ideal accommodation gives it a dark, warm, dry sleeping chamber, a discreet dining and food-storage area hidden from prying eyes below ground, and a vertical surface, well away from its sleeping and dining areas, for relieving itself. A feral ferret (ie one which has escaped or got lost) will create a very similar set-up wherever it finds a suitable retreat. It will have a sleeping corner and a larder and will eat its food within the dark security of its chosen 'burrow'.

There are other requirements induced by confinement for the domesticated animal: security, strict hygiene, plenty of living and exercise space, freedom from draughts and insulation against excessive heat (ferrets are susceptible to heatstroke), interest, and a regular supply of fresh water and fresh food. As the ferret is entirely dependent on you for its accommodation, you must take all these requirements into consideration and you will find plenty of scope for ingenuity in building your own ferret housing. There is little point in trying to buy a readymade ferret hutch these days:

it will be expensive and probably unsuitable unless its maker has a proper knowledge of ferrets. There was a time when there were plenty of well-designed, patented and ingenious ferret hutches on the market in this country but nowadays most people make their own.

Very broadly, then, the most basic ferret housing consists of a dark, enclosed sleeping chamber with access via a small pophole, a small and discreet dining area, a general daylit living area with as much space for exercise as possible, and a latrine area well away from the sleeping and dining end of things. At the very minimum, even a laboratory set-up allows a floor area of 6 sq ft (2 sq m) for two ferrets.

The following description is of an ideal set-up for several ferrets where space, money, time, ingenuity and labour are unlimited. More practical designs are given subsequently!

Take a well-drained area about 10 yds (9 m) square. Make a good frame (wood or metal) and enclose the area with stiff 1-in. (2.5-cm) wire mesh, well-supported, buried at least a yard into the ground and extending two yards above ground so that you can stand comfortably within the enclosure. Extend rustproof mesh horizontally underground at a yard deep and also across the top of the cage. Ferrets love exploring tunnels and holes and are expert at escaping through the smallest outlet; the underground mesh might deter them from digging to freedom. Most of them are not interested in climbing and it may be unnecessary to have overhead mesh, but you can never be sure that an inquisitive or adventurous animal might not find its way out over the top.

A mound of earth will give the ferrets plenty of digging entertainment. You could also supply an artificial warren of pipes, or dig several lengths of interconnecting trenches covered with boards. Slope the trenches for drainage. Some large branches provide something else to be explored, and a variety of hiding places will be popular, such as a pile of logs.

Build a weatherproof, airy but draughtproof shed in one corner of the cage. It must be properly insulated, particularly against hot sun. Ideally it should be in a shady position under trees, or could have climbing plants straggling over the roof if the cage has a wire-mesh top to it. In hot weather it helps to cover an exposed roof with something white to reflect the heat of the sun. Heat can kill ferrets, and can also give breeding problems. Good ventilation is important.

Make sure that there are no mouse-sized potential escape holes at the eaves of the shed. Provide a stable-type door, with a second mesh door so that if the ferrets are confined to the shed they can still have adequate fresh air and light. They should not be kept permanently in semi-darkness.

The floor of the shed must be damp-proof. It should also be scrubbable:

ABOVE: Alec Martin's shed is an ideal commune arrangement, giving his ferrets plenty of space, light and fresh air as well as good security and protection from the weather.   BELOW: Mike Jasper's commune interior: the ferrets have a choice of sleeping and nesting boxes at various levels. Note the thick layer of woodshavings on the floor.

concrete is useful, or brick, and such a floor could be extended beyond the doors to a separately enclosed area outside the shed for restricted access to the great outdoors. Ferrets enjoy a little sun-basking now and then.

In a corner of the cage well away from the shed provide a suitable area for a latrine. Let the animals select the site (they are habitual) and then encourage them to continue to use it by providing a heap of litter and some vertical sheeting, large stones or a tree stump for them to back up against. Alternatively, you could encircle the entire cage with some form of low cladding, perhaps two feet high, which will not only give them a sprainting surface but will also provide draughtproofing, shade and extra protection against the dig to freedom.

Inside the shed have a deep layer of sawdust or other absorbent material on the floor and encourage a latrine corner near the door (so that you can easily get at it for cleaning) and as far as possible from sleeping boxes. Pile the sawdust up into the corner and clear it out regularly to discourage flies and smell. The inside of the shed must be easy to clean. If you paint the whole thing with a non-toxic gloss white paint it will seal off any small crevices where dirt, vermin and bacteria might lurk, so that it will be easier to keep clean and will look fresh and bright. Make a point of giving the whole shed a thorough clean-out at regular intervals with disinfectant, and use anti-parasite dusts on all surfaces, particularly in corners.

Build some shelves inside the shed to support hutches or sleeping boxes. These can be quite simple and restricted if the animals generally have the freedom of the shed, especially if they also have access to the outside cage when you choose. All that is needed are dark enclosed sleeping places with entry through small popholes and access to bedding material. Ferrets often enjoy sleeping together in one box, especially in cold weather, but they should have the option of private quarters.

It may sometimes be necessary to separate an animal from the communal living in the shed and for this purpose you will need hutches adapted from the practical designs in the next section, with sleeping chambers, living areas and latrine corners or sandtrays. Laboratory animals are often kept in single-chamber all-wire cages with no screened-off sleeping area; droppings fall through the mesh floor into a removable metal tray for easy cleaning (so that the assistants do not have to handle the animals), food and water receptacles are hung on the sides of the cages and bedding material is minimal. These cages are stacked in high-rise tiers and the environment is totally controlled, with constant temperatures and humidity, and with a lighting routine to serve the purposes of the researchers. Don't treat your ferrets like lab animals!

The special requirements of nesting jills are considered in Chapter 7.

PRACTICAL HOUSING

The system just described is an elaborate and extensive ferret 'court' for several animals. If you have the space, the court system in one form or another is much the best way of keeping ferrets. It provides them with plenty of living space and fresh air, and it keeps them much fitter and healthier than they would be confined to hutches. It can be scaled down to your available area quite easily.

The old-fashioned ferreters' courts were carefully constructed to provide good exercise and feeding areas with separate sleeping berths, and they allowed selected animals to be separated easily when necessary. Some of our illustrations are based on those in *Ferrets and Ferreting* by the anonymous Editor of *Exchange and Mart*, published in several editions during the first half of this century but now long out-of-print. The small paperback was a classic of its kind and most of its recommendations were very sound indeed.

Figure 3 (a) has two courts and a terrace of six sleeping berths, designed for fifty ferrets, and is solidly built of brick and tile with a sloping concrete floor which could be thoroughly hosed down at intervals. Figure 3 (b) is a four-berth court made from 'champagne boxes with loose lids'! In both these examples the ferrets could readily be separated when necessary, but it is recommended that sick animals or jills in heat or with young should be removed to quite separate quarters in hutches.

You could create an exercise court by enclosing an area adjoining a hutch. It can be as little as 2 ft (60 cm) high if it has a securely meshed roof.

The *Exchange and Mart* book gives several ideas for hutches if you do not have enough space for courts or shed communes. In each case the basic principle is to provide an enclosed and secluded sleeping area, and a living area for feeding and exercise. Figure 4 (c) is slightly more elaborate in that it has a separate third compartment for feeding, with a wooden lip to prevent food being knocked into the wire-floored left-hand compartment used for defecation and limited exercise. An extra refinement would be to separate the latrine area from the exercise area.

With hutches, each area should have a separate access door – access for you, that is. A hinged roof rather than an opening front reduces the risk of the ferrets escaping every time you open the door. It is useful to be able to shut off each compartment internally from the neighbouring area, and with a simple two-chamber system the connecting pophole can have a small shutter-flap.

Exchange and Mart recommends that each hutch should measure 3 ft (1 m) long by 18 ins (45 cm) deep, 18 ins (45 cm) high at the front, with the

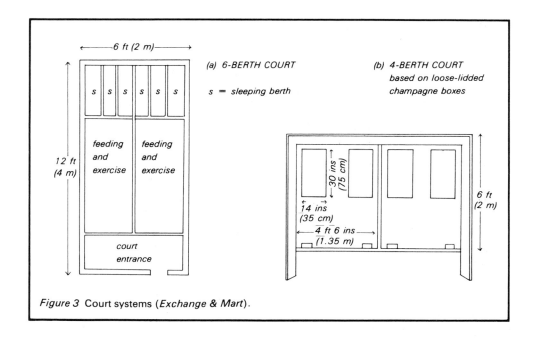

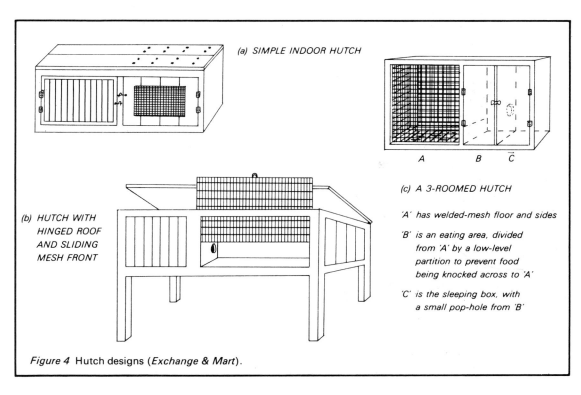

Figure 3 Court systems (*Exchange & Mart*).

(a) 6-BERTH COURT

s = sleeping berth

(b) 4-BERTH COURT
based on loose-lidded
champagne boxes

Figure 4 Hutch designs (*Exchange & Mart*).

(a) SIMPLE INDOOR HUTCH

(b) HUTCH WITH
HINGED ROOF
AND SLIDING
MESH FRONT

(c) A 3-ROOMED HUTCH

'A' has welded-mesh floor and sides

'B' is an eating area, divided
from 'A' by a low-level
partition to prevent food
being knocked across to 'A'

'C' is the sleeping box, with
a small pop-hole from 'B'

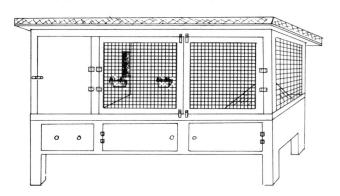

(a)   ACCOMMODATION FOR UP TO
       4 FERRETS

Dimensions: 6 ft x 2 ft x 2 ft
Built of tongue-and-groove
boarding; bitumen roof with
substantial overhang and good
slope. Water and food bowls
hooked onto front mesh.
Latrine corner has glass
'Splashback' plates.

When the hutch is used for a
jill with a litter, glass 6 ins
deep is fitted to the mesh at
floor level for extra security.

(b)   AN INGENIOUS
       OUTDOOR SYSTEM

The hutch can be used as a
linked over-plan arrange-
ment or easily divided into
two units.

There is direct access at
the rear down into the
exercise enclosure at
ground level. The enclosure
could, of course, be
extended indefinitely.

Note the sliding tray for
easy removal of droppings.

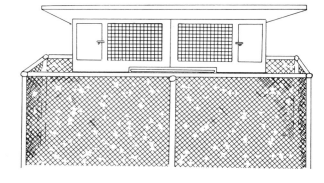

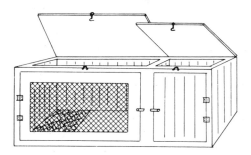

(c)   A SPLIT-LID HUTCH

This gives controlled access
to either section.

Note the coarse-mesh latrine
floor on the left.

Figure 5 Up-to-date hutch ideas.

roof sloping down at the back, and be divided into two compartments. This, they say, would be suitable for two ferrets, although we would prefer such a hutch to be *at least* 4 ft (1.2 m) long. A conventional rabbit hutch is usually 4 ft × 2 ft × 18 ins (1.2 m × 60 cm × 45 cm) and this would certainly be an adequate minimum for two ferrets. However, it would be sensible to limit the depth of the hutch to the length of your own arm in reaching the most inaccessible corner.

Ferrets are gregarious, despite their polecat origins, and in winter they snuggle together in the sleeping quarters. You can thus accommodate more than two in a hutch as long as they have *plenty* of living space. They are active creatures and although they will get exercise during the ferreting months you should remember that for half the year you will not be going ferreting; then they will need either a large hutch area, a separate exercise yard, or a regular walk (they can be trained to walk on a harness and lead as well as any dog). Exercise is important for general health; it also keeps claws in trim and makes life more interesting.

Hutches should be off the ground, partly for your convenience but also to make quite sure that adequate ventilation avoids damp floors, which are certain to lead to footrot, a most unpleasant condition. Outdoor hutches should have plenty of overhang to the roof and the support legs should be creosoted for several inches from ground level to deter pests as much as to make them weatherproof. They should have smaller sleeping compartments so that a pair of ferrets can be really snug in cold weather.

We have illustrated several examples to give you some ideas of what other people have found practical. Ferret keeper John Rainbird paints his hutches inside and out with white gloss paint so that the wood is properly sealed and moisture-repellent. The outside reflects away the heat of any direct sunlight; the white interior not only looks fresh but is also a constant reminder to keep the hutch thoroughly clean. John keeps a hob and jill in this hutch and they have access to a large exercise run. When the jill's litter is due the hob is transferred to a slightly smaller version of the hutch. The jill's hutch is faced with ½-in. (1-cm) mesh to ensure that the kits cannot fall through it.

Veterinary surgeon Dominic Wells gives his ferrets the run of a sheltered, shaded, mesh-fronted garden shed. The mesh is reinforced at ground level for a foot or two because the jills have a monkey-like trick of hanging from the wire and stretching it. They have regular supervised access to the walled garden and this is about the most ideal arrangement we have seen. They use cardboard cartons with lots of bedding for sleeping boxes, which are cheap and disposable so that they are always hygienic. There is plenty to interest the animals as they can see everything that is

John Rainbird's ferret hutch. White gloss paint on the inside gives a fresh look and is an excellent aid to hygiene.

going on in the garden – including the activities of some free-range chickens! There is a small garden pond but neither ferret has ever volunteered for a swim.

MATERIALS

Whether a hutch is kept out-of-doors or in a shed, it is best made with seasoned timber. Wood gives much better insulation than metal, although metal may be easier to keep clean. Use weatherboard or tongue-and-groove, laid horizontally so that there is no inlet for rainwater or draughts. Make sure that internal surfaces are flush (the framework should be outside rather than inside) so that hiding places for vermin, dirt and cached food are minimized. Lining the interior with, say, hardboard helps reduce the hiding places and also gives an extra layer of insulation. If you use plywood the sides and top should be at least $\frac{1}{2}$ in. (13 mm) thick and the floor a more solid $\frac{3}{4}$ in. (2 cm) to prevent warping. Use 2 ins × 4 ins timber for base frames, 2 ins × 2 ins for uprights, and 2 ins × 6 ins for legs (5 cm × 10 cm; 5 cm × 5 cm; 5 cm × 15 cm).

Metal parts, such as nails, screws and catches, must be rustproof (eg brass, but not galvanized) or must be checked regularly to make sure that a rusty screw or catch is not working loose and creating a weak point for escape.

Hutch fronts need strong, welded mesh. Chicken wire is too flexible. 1-in. (2.5-cm) welded mesh is ideal and can also be used for a nursery hutch.

Mesh should be of the square welded type in preference to chicken-wire, which sags. Some people want to be able to make contact with their animals through the mesh but it should not be much more than 1 in. × 1 in. (2.5 cm × 2.5 cm). It is amazing how small a ferret can make itself when there's a possible way out, and its actual solid body is very slim with no broad shoulders or hips to obstruct its passage. Of course, if you expect a jill to raise her young in the cage, the mesh needs to be much smaller. You could use metal rods rather than mesh. But do *not* use anything galvanized: ferrets are susceptible to zinc poisoning and some of them enjoy a good chew on their hutch wire.

If you are using an all-mesh rabbit hutch, the sleeping box must be enclosed with boarding to provide the necessary darkness, warmth and feeling of security.

Outdoor hutches must be weatherproof. Slope the roof from front to back and let it project well beyond the hutch walls (at least 6 ins (15 cm) in each direction). Cover with roofing felt or shingles. Alternatively you could make a free-standing weatherproof roof – a sort of 'hutch port' – to protect several hutches, in which case the overhang should be at least 18 ins (45 cm) beyond the fronts and backs of the hutches and 12 ins (30 cm) beyond the sides. You will of course site the hutches so that the prevailing wind does not drive bad weather in through the mesh fronts.

You can devise a plastic blind to keep out wet weather: hang it from the eaves and weight it with a horizontal batten along the bottom edge which can be hooked into position so that the blind does not flap. For cold dry weather you can use a sacking blind, although you will find that ferrets can take quite a lot of cold weather if they can snuggle together in the sleeping chamber. In hot weather you could use damp sacking but you must remove it at night.

Hutch floors *must* be dry. They can be made of timber but the latrine area will need special attention. However much sand, sawdust or cat litter you use, urine is bound to soak into the wood unless you protect it in some way, either by painting or by lining the favoured corner with rustproof metal or a removable sand tray. (Plastic is too chewable.) A mesh floor for the living area avoids such problems and you can use a sliding tray underneath to make cleaning out simple. A compromise is to carve out just the relevant corner of a wooden floor and replace it with firmly affixed mesh. You could bore holes in the wood for drainage but remember how attractive holes are to ferrets.

It is fortunate that ferrets are such clean animals and that they are very careful to defecate in the same corner every time, as far away from their food and their nest as they can get. Even a sick animal will make an effort to use that corner. If you feed them properly the droppings are hard and easy to remove, but if you give them bread and milk, for example, or too much fat and eggs, the droppings will be much looser and more difficult to deal with.

Ferret keepers are always ingenious and have been known to make ferret housing from old kitchen units, packing cases and anything else that comes to hand. *Exchange and Mart* recommends potato barrels, especially as emergency housing for sick ferrets. The circular ends of the barrel rest on wooden projections 3 ins (8 cm) from each end and 'when you want to clean it out, invert the barrel – the ferret or ferrets having been previously removed – scrape the end and set the barrel up again in a reversed position. In this way it will keep sweet and dry a very long time.' Whatever you use, it is certainly a good idea to have emergency accommodation available and it is also useful to make a carrying box of some kind, even if you never go ferreting, so that you have some chance of catching that escaped ferret when the occasion arises.

SECURITY

It is essential that accommodation should be ferretproof. Ferrets will wreak havoc in a chicken-house or pigeon-loft and will terrify caged rabbits. An escaped ferret can cause mayhem and is likely to have a short life: it will be knocked off by a frightened neighbour who knows nothing about ferrets (or even that it *is* a ferret), or by an irate poultry owner, a gamekeeper, unfamiliar traffic, or a persistent terrier. The greatest enemy of wild polecats and escaped ferrets alike is Man and it is your responsibility to protect your ferret from such a predator or his agents by ensuring that your hutches, courts, sheds and runs are one hundred per cent secure.

Check regularly and thoroughly for the beginnings of any small hole ($1\frac{1}{2}$ ins (4 cm) is big enough for some ferrets). Fit a double system of catches to every door. If you use butterfly catches it is essential to back them up with a second catch, such as a small bolt, because a bored ferret is quite capable of working at a toggle or a hook and eye until it opens, by chance or by intent – and a ferret is quite intelligent enough to do so by intent. A really dozy albino might feel that the subsequent jump down to ground level is too risky but he will find a way down soon enough. Freedom is always worthy of investigation.

Be particularly alert during the mating season when even the tamest housepet jill may have a strong urge to wander off. If she does so, her chances of coming across a mate are remote; although quite a number of ferrets escape or are not retrieved from a lie-up, they either succumb quickly to Man or they are so widely dispersed that lack of opportunity leads to breeding failure. It seems to be only on islands that a feral ferret population sometimes builds up – for example there have been known populations from time to time on Mull, Bute and Cumbrae.

Allowing a ferret to escape does no favours to anyone, and certainly not to the ferret itself. Ferrets also get stolen, despite the fact that they can be bought so reasonably. We have heard of some distressing cases of vandalism involving something far more vicious than simply releasing ferrets, so it might be wise to protect your animals with padlocks in some circumstances.

BEDDING
Supply ample fresh bedding material so that the ferret can drag as much as it wants into its sleeping compartment, particularly in winter or in the nesting season when the bedding will probably be piled up so plentifully that there seems to be little room for the ferret. An expectant jill is very thorough in her nest-making and often heaps the bedding up to the top of the chamber, leaving just a small entrance hole.

The bedding material can be straw, hay, shredded paper, wood shavings or similar substances, depending on circumstances and sources of supply. Bear the following points in mind.

Straw should for preference be clean wheat or oat straw. Barley straw is softer but it tends to contain a lot of dust and loose barley awns (whiskers). Awns have been known to cause abscesses. Good straw is a well-ventilated and very suitable bedding material.

Hay must have been well made and properly dried. It should be sweet-smelling without any hint of mildew or mustiness. We have had reports of hayseeds lodging in various orifices of ferrets' anatomies and causing abscesses in the same way that barley awns can. Hay should not be used for a jill with a litter because the young can suffocate in its softness, or can become so overheated that they literally stick together. Nor should hay be used in summer for adults: the warmth of it may give them the 'sweats', which can kill.

Shredded paper must be free of toxics – some printing inks are undesirable – and should not be used for young litters as the kits may become entangled in it.

Wood chips can be used – cedar ones would produce a pleasant smell – but very occasionally a ferret might inadvertently swallow a piece which could lodge in its throat. Nor do wood chips stay snugly in place when a ferret makes its bed.

Whichever material you choose, the sleeping chamber could benefit from a $1\frac{1}{2}$-ins (4-cm) base layer of sawdust or wood chips for extra insulation.

To avoid any build-up of pests, clean out old bedding regularly (say weekly) and provide fresh material. But make exceptions in the case of a nursing jill: her nest should not be disturbed for several weeks.

LITTER

Litter can be spread on the floor outside the sleeping area and a good pile of it should be heaped in the latrine corner. You can use materials like sand, sawdust, dry ashes, peat moss, calcined clay, vermiculite or petshop litter. The point of the litter is to absorb moisture and odour and to make for easier cleaning out. Your job will be simpler if you clean out regularly. Daily removal of the corner pile is ideal, or perhaps three times a week, once a week at the outside. The floor must be kept dry and clean to avoid footrot and other diseases.

As ferrets are so careful in their habits, they will soon learn to use a litter tray and this will make cleaning out a quick daily job. The tray should be large and deep enough to retain the litter and should be placed in a corner so that they have something to back up against.

CLEANING OUT

Some people honestly believe that cleaning out a ferret's living quarters is bad for the ferret. Their theory is that hardiness is only achieved by exposure, ie that a dirty hutch breeds resistance to disease and that hygiene breeds weakness and susceptibility. None of them have asked their ferrets whether they prefer to live in dank dirty hutches.

In the wild the polecat (like the badger) keeps its burrow clean, as already described. Given the choice, therefore, it opts for hygiene. In captivity that choice should be respected.

Wild animals are regular and predictable in their habits (so are most human beings) and domesticated animals appreciate regular routines. If you clean out regularly, it is not so much a chore as a simple routine that takes a few minutes, and if you clean out on the same day of the week you will not forget how long it was since the last time. Remove soiled litter and hidden food daily; clean out the living area three times a week; change bedding materials once a week; dust hutches with anti-parasite powder occasionally; and scrub hutches and sheds from top to bottom regularly. Better still, devise your own timetable – and stick to it!

A propane torch makes a thorough job of cleaning woodwork and wire and can get at seams and corners.

FIXTURES AND FITTINGS
Food and water containers should *not* be galvanized because of the risk of zinc poisoning. If containers are placed on the floor or ground they must be heavy and broad-based. Ferrets are endlessly inquisitive and playful animals and will certainly push them around and tip them over if they can. For the same reason, wall-mounted containers must be firmly fixed. A wall-mounted drinking system is particularly useful because a floor water-bowl is bound to result in a soaked floor.

You could use a heavy cast-iron saucepan or frying pan without a handle, but it might be difficult to keep clean. You can buy good earthenware food bowls from pet shops; designed for dogs and cats, they have broad bases and are well weighted, with glazed surfaces so that they are easy to clean, and they are ideal if you are feeding anything other than whole carcases. Plastic bowls are useless for ferrets.

Pet shops can also supply a variety of drinkers or you can devise your own system with a little imagination. The basics are that the main water reservoir is outside the hutch or cage, for easy filling, with a drinking mechanism of some kind inside. Hygiene is important and you should check that all parts of the drinking system can be cleaned easily and are always working properly. Ferrets need access to *fresh* cool drinking-water at all times, and will be particularly thirsty on a raw meat diet. Check that they have learned how to use a water-bottle system and until you are certain give them a drink from a bowl as well at feeding or exercise time.

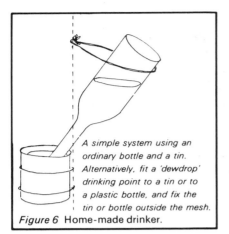

A simple system using an ordinary bottle and a tin. Alternatively, fit a 'dewdrop' drinking point to a tin or to a plastic bottle, and fix the tin or bottle outside the mesh.

Figure 6 Home-made drinker.

ABOVE: Floor-standing bowls must be heavy and have broad bases. Ferrets cannot resist a challenge: if they can tip something over they will. An alternative is to use containers that hook firmly on the mesh; they cannot be dislodged and the contents are less likely to be knocked to the floor. LEFT: Water bowls on the hutch floor are an invitation to chaos. Pet shops sell simple drinking systems, with a water bottle safely outside the hutch to keep the water contained and clean. There are various types of drinker mechanisms which protrude into the hutch through the mesh but you must be sure that your ferrets learn how to use them properly. A constant supply of fresh drinking-water is essential.

PESTS

Flies may be a problem, especially if you are less than scrupulous at removing hidden food (ferrets, like wild polecats, have a great urge to 'cache' food) and clearing out scats and litter. In a shed you can use fly-paper, keeping it well out of reach of the ferrets. We have not heard of problems with insecticidal devices but feel that they might not be a good idea in the restricted space of a shed.

Fleas and other parasites will find a refuge in hutches and shed, and you will not eradicate them if you only dust the ferrets. Dust every corner of the accommodation at regular intervals and change and burn bedding frequently.

5 Feeding

Wild polecats are carnivores. They are known to catch and eat a wide variety of prey, and a typical diet (calculated from the methodical examination of the contents of 250 polecats' stomachs in Britain, Czechoslovakia and Russia) is composed as follows:

Mammals	35–71%
Birds	6–14%
Amphibians and reptiles	9–26%
Fish	0–14%
Invertebrates	0–24%

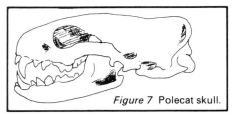

Figure 7 Polecat skull.

The mammals, which form the greatest percentage of the diet, include rabbits, hares, mice, rats, voles, shrews, hedgehogs and moles. Small birds are eaten and birds' eggs are a favourite treat. The amphibians and reptiles include lizards, snakes (even adders), frogs (sometimes stored alive but paralysed by a bite at the base of the skull so that the prey stays fresh for quite some time in winter) and occasionally toads. Eels are also taken, along with worms, slugs, insects and spiders.

Polecats like a fresh meal, but they often store a kill (and usually forget it) or take carrion if they come across it. They are efficient killers. They stalk the prey and strike suddenly, sinking their long canine teeth sharply into the back of the victim's neck. Mink also use this method of biting at the base of the skull behind the ear and into the brain, killing very quickly indeed. If the first bite does not kill immediately, the polecat will crush a small victim with its cheek teeth and shake it to break its neck. Larger prey are either killed by the base-of-the-brain attack or by a bite at the jugular vein so that the victim rapidly bleeds to death. Polecats are as fearless as terriers and are unusual among carnivores in that they are capable of catching and killing, without any assistance, prey which is considerably larger than they are themselves. The average weight of a wild polecat is a couple of pounds and the average healthy rabbit weighs three or four pounds. Nor is the rabbit incapable of self-defence; its back feet are very powerful and can cause raking gashes on an enemy.

Small prey (up to mouse size) is eaten whole, bones, fur, feathers and all. With larger prey some bones are eaten but the skull and any long bones are discarded, as is the skin. The roughage elements of fur, feather and bone are an important part of the diet: the polecat's gut is very short and it is not able to digest vegetable matter, which tends to pass straight through the system. The natural roughage of fur and feather aids digestion, giving the muscles something to work on, and also helps to clean the animal's teeth. The bone content adds valuable supplements to the diet, particularly calcium.

A ferret's nutritional requirements are, of course, similar to the pole-cat's. Ferrets are carnivores and they are probably healthiest on a fresh 'whole-carcase' diet. If they are fed only meat – without fur, feather and bone – the diet will be lacking in certain respects and will need to be supplemented, particularly with vitamin E and calcium. The aim in feeding a ferret is to provide a balanced, nutritional and palatable diet, with a little variety not just for interest but also to ensure that the diet *is* balanced. However, dietary changes should always be introduced gradually to avoid digestive upsets.

There are several practical snags to whole-carcase diets. We are certainly not suggesting that you feed live prey to a ferret, but you must ensure that the carcase is fresh (or thoroughly thawed if it was frozen while fresh). It might be difficult to obtain a regular supply of fresh carcases and there is also a risk that they carry disease or parasites. Fortunately there are plenty of alternatives to whole-carcase diets, although it is beneficial to the ferret if it does receive two whole-carcase meals a week within the context of the rest of its diet.

Animal nutritionists have made close studies of the requirements of the American mink, *Mustela vison*, because of course mink farming can be a profitable business. Ferret nutrition has not been so carefully investigated, because on the whole no one makes substantial profits from ferrets nor has any pet-food manufacturer in this country yet found enough of a market to make it worthwhile producing ferret food. However, for those who are interested in the science of nutrition, we have included two nutrition tables in Part II. One is recommendations for mink (p. 173), and the other is a guide produced for New Zealand fitch farmers (p. 174).

The ferret diet should have a high protein content. Protein is essential for its vigour, growth and good coat, and in an animal with such a high metabolic rate a continual input of protein is very important. Protein is available from both animal and vegetable sources but a carnivore's gut is adapted to make the most of 'higher' (ie animal) protein. A ferret's diet should contain an average of at least 30 per cent animal protein and perhaps 20 per cent animal fat. An 'Original Ferret Diet' was at one stage developed in the United States in response to the increasing population of pet ferrets and it was based on a ratio of 32 per cent protein and 20 per cent fat; it seemed to provide a healthy diet on its own, with a claim that it also reduced the ferret's muskiness and resulted in less smelly droppings.

We have been unable to obtain details of this product's contents so can make no recommendations about it.

The main point you need to bear in mind is that ferrets are carnivores. The wild polecat lives largely on meat, although it will happily snaffle a few berries occasionally. It does not eat grass, nor does it chew on grain, nor does it have the luxury of milk once it has been weaned. All of which is to say that the old bread-and-milk diet so favoured by ferreters is *not* suitable for ferrets except as an occasional treat or emergency snack when nothing else is available. Milk can cause scouring to a greater or lesser degree and that means loose and smelly droppings. Some ferret keepers might be surprised to learn that a healthy ferret's droppings are firm, even hard, like those of most wild carnivores. A feral ferret's droppings are just over an inch long, twisted, tapered at the end, and black. Droppings are a good indication of an animal's health and the adequacy of its diet.

The foods you might find suitable and convenient are considered a little later on but first of all what about when, how and how much to feed?

There are many conflicting views on how often you should feed a ferret, ranging from several times a day in an ideal world to 'whenever I remember', which is an unforgivably irresponsible attitude towards an animal that is dependent on its keeper. We have already mentioned that regular routines are important, not only because animals are creatures of habit but also because routines ensure that a faulty memory does not have a part to play. It is probably more important that you should devise your own feeding timetable, so that you will stick to it, than that we should lay down any hard-and-fast ideas for you, but the best routine is to feed twice a day every day. Then the food will always be fresh so that you reduce the problem of flies etc. (always remove uneaten food, especially hoards); the ferret will have something to occupy its time and it will have the comfortable familiarity and security of a routine. Little and often is even better than twice a day. Some people feed every other day but that is not to be recommended and a bulky carcase thrown in to last for a week is not recommended at all.

The next question is: 'How much?' Ferrets normally eat to their caloric requirement; most of them know when to stop and if you give them as much as they will clear up then and there you will not go far wrong. But keep an eye on it – healthy animals are fit, not fat. A reasonable dry-matter intake would be on average an ounce or two a day, but there are so many variables to take into account that averages are not much help. There is such a range of sizes and bodyweights in ferrets. Then there is the time of year: piling on the fat and fur for the winter, building up a pregnant jill's reserves and replenishing what she loses during nursing and maternal stress, the varying appetites in the breeding season, a loss of appetite in hot weather, and so on. Sometimes a ferret's appetite reduces for no apparent reason, but there is probably no cause for concern – it's just an off day. In the wild it may fail to find prey every day.

If you keep several ferrets together it is worth making sure that a weaker animal is getting its fair share of food. Competition seems to stimulate a healthy appetite, incidentally, and a ferret kept alone may eat much better if it has to bicker a little for its food.

The hoarding habit is very ferret. Excessive hoarding may mean that an animal is nervous of something – perhaps of you or a fellow ferret. A pregnant jill is likely to build up her larder in preparation for the imminent kits. However, hoarded food is as often as not left uneaten – it is a habit rather than a need, like a dog burying a bone – and you must remove it before the maggots start breeding, especially in summer. If you feed little and often, and *regularly*, hoarding should be greatly reduced.

We have heard an imaginative theory that hoarding of some foods, particularly milk-soaked bread, is an indication of a lack in the diet and that the ferret 'allows' the hoard to ferment so that whatever was lacking is then made available to it by the activity of various micro-organisms. The ferret's gut does not harbour the necessary microflora to break down vegetable fibre, for example, so there just might be something in this theory.

Whole-carcase food can be given quite literally whole, especially if it is small enough – for example a mouse or a day-old chick. A whole rabbit or rook is far too much for one ferret to eat fresh, and raw food (which is preferable to cooked) can quickly become a source of infection. Mink farmers and gamekeepers often grind up whole carcases through a strong mincer – bones, flesh, fur and all. This practice should ensure that there is no risk of damage from bone shards lodging in the ferret's throat or gut and at the same time it supplies an excellent balanced diet. Carcases can be deep frozen when they are fresh (whole or minced) but they must be thawed properly at normal room temperatures before being fed. Mincers must be kept scrupulously clean, with every tiny corner being thoroughly scrubbed and sterilized.

Feeding whole-carcase meals once or twice a week, with other food for the rest of the week, is sound practice: it keeps the ferret's digestive system in good order as well as providing the necessary vitamins and minerals that may be lacking in other diets. Try to feed at least *some* raw meat every day, in one form or another. If you keep a lot of ferrets, it is worth contacting the Fur Breeders Association for advice on bulk-ration mixing.

A balanced diet is probably best achieved if it offers variety. Now let's take a look at possible foods.

Tripe is a good food for ferrets. Alec Martin feeds it raw to his animals.

Wild animals and birds

Bearing in mind the polecat's normal diet, a ferret can thrive on the carcases of all manner of wild creatures. Ferret keepers are frequently seen
furtively collecting 'road mashes' but you must be a little careful in your
gleaning. For example, a normally agile and alert species like a cat might
have been knocked down because it was not in the best of health. Many
wild animals will harbour intestinal worms. Avoid anything that shows the
slightest signs of decomposition because ferrets are particularly susceptible
to botulism. If you come across a dead mouse or rat, treat it with extreme
caution as it might well have been poisoned. Some ferrets, while quite
happy to eat rats, much prefer mice given the choice and two mice a day
per ferret is a regular diet for lab ferrets. Rabbit nearly always goes down

well and there is no need to listen to those who say that if you feed rabbit to a ferret you will ruin it as a bolter of rabbits.

Poultry

If you have a source of day-old chicks culled from a hatchery, make the most of it. Hatcheries that sell egg-laying pullets (as opposed to table birds) only want hen chicks. Half the eggs are likely to hatch out as cockerel chicks and they are killed as soon as their sex is known. Day-old chicks are an ideal food for ferrets, but not to the exclusion of other foods.

You might also find a source of table-bird waste – chicken heads, necks, guts and so on – but mink farms are quick to snap up these. Poultry offal is a good source of protein, fat and minerals and it can form up to 60 per cent of a ferret's diet some of the time. But beware! Many a ferret has become sterile through eating capon heads and it is best to avoid poultry waste in the breeding season. Nor, for other reasons, should you give pregnant or nursing jills too much poultry. Note too that poultry offal is readily attacked by bacteria and it requires careful pre-cooling before freezing, with equally careful and thorough defrosting before feeding.

Laboratory culls

Another useful food source for ferrets is surplus rats and mice from a laboratory, as long as you are certain that they have not been pumped full of unpleasantries.

Slaughterhouse and butcher by-products

Raw green tripe is excellent for ferrets, if you can get it. Other possibilities are sheep paunch, lungs (lights), udders, cheek flaps, tongues etc, but so much is now bought up by pet-food manufacturers that it has become quite expensive. If you do find a supply, make quite sure it is fresh when you feed it.

Offal

Liver is a good source of protein, vitamins, trace minerals and essential fatty acids, and it is an important element in the diet of pregnant and nursing jills and their growing youngsters. However, liver is said to contain 'unknown growth factors' and in excess it would also give too much vitamin A. It should not constitute a major proportion of any diet but it is certainly beneficial to include a little liver regularly.

You may find that the only cattle or sheep liver available has been condemned as unfit for human consumption because of liver fluke and this should be avoided. You could, however, use pigs' liver which has been rejected because of 'milk spots', but not if it has been condemned for any other reason.

If you can find a cheap source of brains, heart, kidneys and spleens, so much the better. All offal should be very fresh and should be fed raw. It is still possible for tuberculosis to be passed to a ferret from infected offal but if you deal with a licensed slaughterer this will not be a risk.

Meat

Frozen 'pet mince' is a useful standby. Defrost it thoroughly. Once defrosted it should be fed immediately; it usually has a high proportion of offal and the bacteria soon get to work. Also, rancid fat can cause metabolic problems.

If you are feeding an all-meat diet, so that the ferret is not getting any bone, fur or feather, you must supplement with vitamin E. Vitamin E deficiency can contribute to various metabolic disorders such as rickets, anaemia, yellow fat disease and inability to produce milk. The deficiency is more pronounced if the diet is high in PUFA (polyunsaturated fatty acids) because PUFA places demands on vitamin E reserves. Reduce PUFA levels if you can, or protect the reserves by including an antioxidant in the ration, and in any event include a stabilized vitamin E supplement at the rate of 10-20 mg per day (10 mg with any meat diet, and 20-30 mg for a high-PUFA diet). Lactating jills need at least 5 per cent fresh liver in their ration; indeed a little liver in any ferret's diet should safeguard vitamin E levels. PUFA levels are high in things like oily fish, chicken offal, horse meat and slink meat (aborted or premature calves). Something like mutton has lower PUFA levels.

All-meat diets are also deficient in calcium, which is an essential element for all animals, particularly if they are growing fast. Calcium is needed for healthy teeth and bones. Milk is a good source, in limited quantities (see below), or you can add 5-10 per cent of fresh ground bone in the meat diet or 2 per cent of bonemeal, which is available from chemists but you should make it clear that it is for feeding to an animal rather than for the garden! Jills giving milk definitely need a calcium supplement.

Cereals and milk

Ferrets cannot digest cereals unless the grain has been thoroughly crushed and cooked. Flaked cereals (oats, wheat, maize) are acceptable, also dog biscuits (preferably puppy meal), soya bean products (soya is not a cereal but it is an excellent source of vegetable protein) and so on. Cereals are not necessary if you are feeding whole carcases occasionally, but they can be useful as a basis for vitamin and mineral supplements. The grain germ is a good source of vitamin E for pregnant jills. Cereals should not form more than 10 per cent of any ration and, if you do feed them, introduce them gradually into the diet or the ferret might suffer from bloat, otherwise known as 'stomach overload'!

Bread is of course cereal. It is possible to feed ferrets on a bread-and-milk diet, especially if you add a little margarine to it, and they will get plenty of protein and calcium, but it is *not* recommended except in an emergency or as a warm meal for a sick animal which is off its food. There used to be two reasons for keeping ferrets on bread-and-milk: one was that it was cheap, and the second was a theory that if you fed any kind of meat to a working ferret it would become a bloodthirsty killer and would therefore 'kill down' and 'lie up' in the bury rather than bolting out the rabbits. That theory has long since been shown to be entirely false, as is the theory that ferrets should be starved before working. More about that in Chapter 8.

The ferret's digestive system is not designed for a bread-and-milk diet and this is made very evident by the loose and smelly droppings it produces. It will also give rise to teeth problems: ferrets need something to chew on for strong teeth and healthy gums.

Milk is, however, a useful source of calcium and ferrets love it! So give it as a treat but not as a substantial proportion of the diet. If you water down the milk, the laxative effect will be reduced. Tinned evaporated (not condensed) milk is a useful standby, and half a tin of evap plus a pint of fresh skim milk with four scalded slices of bread will do seven ferrets nicely.

Fish

Fish can be fed occasionally but avoid salted, cured or very oily fish. Certain fish contain thiaminase which if fed in any quantities can cause thiamine deficiency in a ferret. Herring, mullet, sprats, dogfish, squid, carp, crabs and mussels are possible sources of thiaminase. White fish such as cod, flat fish and whiting can be fed quite safely but whiting and hake guts should be removed before feeding. Be careful with fish bones, which could easily lodge in a ferret's mouth, throat or guts.

Eggs

Ferrets love eggs but they should only be an occasional treat, say once a week. Too much egg can lead to baldness but this might be avoided if you boil the eggs for fifteen minutes. A whole raw egg in its shell will give a ferret plenty of entertainment as well as a gourmet treat.

A raw egg is an appreciated snack – but not too often.

Prepared foods

Ferrets can be given tinned dog or cat foods within reason. Cheap and cheerful 'Chappie' seems to be better than some of the more expensive dog foods, even though it has a fairly high cereal content. If the droppings look loose and lurid, reduce the tinned food and replace it with fresh meat, which is anyway preferable. Kitten food is ideal for growing youngsters.

If you feed nothing but cat food you may end up with breeding problems because the ferret's protein intake can become too low. Dry cat foods and 'chows' can be fed as long as plenty of fresh drinking water is always available. Dry food does give the ferret something to exercise its teeth on but we would not recommend a diet of nothing but dry food. Supplement it with fresh liver or give fresh meat or tinned pet food twice a week.

Commercial wet or dry mink foods are a possibility if you can get them. The British mink industry experimented with 'complete' dry foods for mink some years ago but discarded them in the late 1970s. However, research into this subject is actively continuing in North America and Scandinavia and the Fur Breeders Association will be able to give up-to-date information for large-scale ferretries. Zoos also use specially formulated foods for their mustelids and some ferrets have been fed on a moistened dry cat diet 'in a porridge form' – which does not sound very exciting for the ferret.

Laboratory ferrets in Britain are often given pelleted diets, which are convenient and hygienic. Dr John Hammond Jr, who has cared for some

1,800 ferrets, uses pig-weaning pellets containing 23 per cent protein, 7.5 per cent fat and 1.5 per cent fibre. However, he is careful to avoid products which contain copper, a supplement often added to pig diets for growth. He has also tried a patented 'Lab Diet for Rodents' (21.3 per cent protein, 3.4 per cent fat, 2.2 per cent fibre). Both diets are based on mixed cereals plus fish meal, added fat, and vitamin and mineral supplements. Milk powder and antibiotics are also included. The pellets are particularly useful for kits: they can be fed a warm 'wet mash' from 20 days old to weaning at 7 weeks old. Although the young prefer dry pellets, their jaws do not seem to be strong enough to cope with them. Dry pellets are not hoarded like fresh food. Dr Hammond advises caution with fishmeal products because if they are based on herrings preserved in nitrates the pellet-making process may give rise to carcinogens, which can cause tumours in ferrets. Processed groundnut products may also induce tumours.

Supplements

The main deficiencies to guard against are vitamin E and calcium, and they can be avoided by including liver and bonemeal in the diet. Pregnant and nursing jills have special requirements: add small quantities of ordinary salt to a jill's ration (up to 0.05 per cent of her whole ration) from May onwards to avoid 'nursing sickness', but too much salt in any diet can be toxic.

Dietary supplements should only be added where necessary and in moderation. It is possible to overdo it: excessive vitamin A, for example, can result in loss of fur. If you are using dog or cat supplements, make allowances for the comparatively small bodyweight of the ferret and reduce amounts accordingly.

The vegetarian ferret

A certain member of a certain ferret club is a vegetarian, and so are his ferrets, but we have no details of the diet nor of the health of his animals. We do know that he is a caring ferret keeper and would therefore adjust the diet if he thought it was in the interests of his animals.

Snacks and titbits

The diets of pet ferrets can be supplemented with household scraps but bear in mind that at least half the ferret's total food intake should be of animal rather than vegetable origin. Avoid sweet foods, whole grains and highly seasoned foods. Scraps can add welcome variety, especially if you normally feed convenience foods such as tinned or dry pet foods. A good marrow bone every now and then will be appreciated and it will help supply calcium and phosphorus as well as keeping the ferret's teeth in good condition.

Ferrets have their own fancies and we have heard of a lot of strange tastes: icecream, cake, cheese, chocolate, grapes, bananas, worms, beetles, carrots, sultanas, celery, prunes and even melon rinds. Ferrets need not be deprived of some of the interesting tastes and textures of foods other than meat – in moderation!

WATER

Ferrets need access to fresh drinking-water at all times, even when they are given milk at feeding time They will of course be particularly thirsty in warm weather, and also if they are on a raw-meat diet. It is essential that lactating jills have as much water as they want. Working ferrets have been known to travel quite a long way in search of water and this is one cause of the disappearing ferret!

6 Maintenance and Health

Given a fair chance, ferrets are tough healthy animals. Poor management, inappropriate feeding or a lack of understanding of the animal's needs are the most likely causes of health problems. Heredity plays a part too, but that comes under the heading of poor management because it can be minimized by careful breeding.

Good management makes for healthy animals and if you follow our guidelines on housing, feeding and breeding you will have a sound basis. There are a few regular maintenance routines that will help keep it that way.

Teeth

Ferrets can suffer from abscesses of one kind or another and these are often found in or around the jaw. It helps if you keep your animal's teeth clean and check them at intervals for any signs of trouble, such as small fragments of bone lodging between tooth and gum. Some people use a smoker's toothpaste, rubbing the teeth with a clean handkerchief, to keep

Tooth inspection! A light pinch on the forehead encourages a ferret to open wide. A well-handled ferret will not bite even if you put your fingers into its mouth.

tartar in check. Regular treatment of this kind also makes sure the ferret is used to having fingers in its mouth and your vet might thank you for that one day!

Everyone has their own techniques for persuading a ferret to open wide – a slight pressure on the jaw-hinge, or a light pinch on the skin between the ears. You can use a wooden spatula (eg an ice-lolly stick) to depress its lower jaw. If your ferret is well-handled you should have no problem in persuading it to open its mouth enough for tooth inspection and treatment.

Chewing – whether on bones, meat or the wire of a cage – can sometimes loosen the teeth enough to make a convenient nest for bacteria in the gums. This is how many abscesses start and how teeth can begin to rot, so pay special attention to the gums. On the other hand, a 'soft' diet can also produce tooth problems; if you give the occasional whole-carcase meal the roughage helps clean the teeth and get rid of any residual soft food and germs between teeth and gums. It also provides calcium, which is good for teeth, especially in the growing youngster.

Claws

Unlike cats, ferrets have non-retractile claws and they can grow quite long, particularly in pets. Working ferrets sometimes *need* their claws and it is usually unnecessary to clip them. Regular exercise, even on grass, helps to keep claws in trim. Use dog or cat nail-clippers for trimming and take care not to cut near the sensitive quick. If you make it bleed, draw a bar of softened soap across to staunch it.

Coat

Ferrets do not need brushing and combing, although some of them enjoy grooming. They moult periodically, as described in Chapter 2. Bathing is not necessary, unless you are advised to use a special shampoo against parasites. A few ferrets enjoy an occasional voluntary splashabout, but most do not like the indignity of being doused and shampooed.

A drink of cold tea twice a week keeps the coat in good condition, and an occasional treat of a beaten egg helps too. Albinos may go very yellow in the breeding season because of the activity of their sebaceous glands.

Eyes

Most eye problems are accidental, like scratches from brambles. Weepy eyes might be a sign of distemper, especially if the eyelids are gummed-up. Unvaccinated ferrets are very susceptible to distemper, which is a killer.

Ears

Check the ears regularly, but do not poke around inside them. Ferrets do not normally have visible ear wax and if you see signs of what you think is wax it could be an indication of ear mites or infection, particularly if the animal is constantly scratching at its ears, shaking its head or holding its head a little to one side. All ferrets scratch and shake their head a bit – it is as habitual as humans yawning or running their fingers through their hair – but watch out for *un*usual behaviour. Treatment for ear problems is given in the Vet Check section in Part II. Unless you are quite sure you know what you are doing, do not poke around with cotton buds to clean out a ferret's ears.

Feet

In the bad old days many ferrets suffered from 'footrot', a very unpleasant condition in which the feet became sore, swollen and scabby. In bad cases the claws dropped out. (Swollen feet can also be a sign of distemper if other typical signs of that disease are present – see below.)

Footrot is the result of damp and dirty living conditions, something like trench foot. It can be due to bacteria or to a mite but if you look after your animals you should never see the problem. It is important that hutch floors should be dry and clean.

Check feet regularly anyway and always clean and dry them immediately after a day's ferreting or after exercising, particularly between the toes.

HEALTH PROBLEMS

For many reasons, ferrets are not often seen in veterinary practices and some vets are unfamiliar with them – uncertain how to approach and handle them, convinced that they will stink out the surgery, and perhaps unaware of some of the ferret's special requirements.

It is a vicious circle. Traditionally, ferret keepers do not consult vets, partly because of the cost, partly because they prefer to consult other ferret keepers, and partly because of the false belief that caring is somehow 'soft' and that nature should be allowed to take its course. Whatever the reasons, the result is that vets are denied familiarity with ferrets unless they happen to keep some themselves (quite a few do) or have been approached by local ferret clubs or pet owners. Some vets become particularly interested in ferrets; the pages of *The Veterinary Record* often carry details of their experiences, and those who are interested know whom to consult about ferrets.

If your own vet knows only that ferrets can on the whole be treated much like a cat, he might need a little more information. We have therefore included a separate section in Part II of this book which has been written in consultation with veterinary surgeons well qualified in the treatment of ferrets and whose names are familiar within the profession. Ferret keepers will not need the technical information in the Vet Check section and will probably never come across most (if any) of the problems discussed, but we have tried to give comprehensive details for the sake of reference. Don't let the catalogue put you off: ferrets are tough! We have met people who have cared for very large numbers and hardly ever had an illness in any of them, yet someone else with just two or three might be unfortunate enough to have problems that no one else has even heard of. A lot of it is knowing your ferret, but some of it is sheer bad luck. Like any other animal, some ferrets seem to have been programmed for trouble.

It is important to be on good terms with your vet and to have faith in his judgment. Do not make his job more difficult by making your own diagnosis and do make use of his professional services sooner rather than later. Ferrets tend to show little sign of an illness until it is well advanced and then they often succumb very suddenly so that fast action is vital. If your vet knows you already and knows that you keep ferrets, he will be better prepared in the case of an emergency. Even the most observant and caring owners have had their ferrets dying on them without warning and for no obvious reason. There is still a great deal to be learned about ferrets; after all these centuries of domestication very little is really known about them. In the past they were taken for granted and were considered no great loss if they died. Fortunately more and more people are now taking an interest in them and the veterinary profession is being helped by laboratory investigators as well as caring ferret keepers. In New Zealand, where fitch farming is seen to have commercial potential, there has been a sudden surge of interest in the wellbeing of ferrets: it is amazing how the promise of profit can stimulate concern.

The rest of this chapter is devoted to problems in layman terms. Veterinary surgeons should refer to the Vet Check section and to the detailed Ferret Facts table in Part II.

CONVENIENCE SURGERY

Sometimes people have things done to their animals for the sake of convenience or prevention rather than to relieve pain, cure an illness or save a life. Whether or not such operations are in the interests of the animal itself could be debatable. They are usually to do with controlling reproduction (castration, vasectomy and spaying) or purely cosmetic (removal of scent glands). Some veterinary surgeons are understandably reluctant to undertake such operations, for ethical reasons, and you, too, should listen to your conscience. Any operation, however minor, on any creature, carries an element of risk.

Castration

Castration of the male ferret is of advantage to the pet owner because it reduces the male's seasonal aggressiveness and desire to wander, and it also reduces to some extent his musky smell. For the pet owner, those three reasons may be enough.

Castration is best carried out at 6–8 months of age under general anaesthetic.

Vasectomy

Successful vasectomy renders the male ferret infertile but does not reduce his sexual urges or performance in any way. It can be a convenient method of birth control if you prefer to keep a hob and jill together – the hob can go through all the motions and the jill will be brought out of oestrus (see Chapter 7) but will not of course produce a litter.

Spaying

Spaying involves the removal of a jill's womb so that she can never again become pregnant. It is a very final operation and you must be quite certain that you will never want to breed from her in the future. It involves a flank incision under general anaesthetic, and you should bear in mind that any general anaesthetic carries its own risk, however slight. You might prefer to use the hormonal 'jill jab' or 'jill pill' as a method of birth control (see Vet Check). Spaying does not seem to alter a jill's personality much, although she may put on weight and her coat markings might alter after the next moult. The best age for spaying is 6–8 months.

When weighing up whether to spay or not to spay, remember that prolonged oestrus (ie being in season for some time without being mated) can lead to all sorts of problems with some jills, as described in the Breeding chapter, and that hormonal treatment might possibly have long-term effects that are not yet properly understood. There are several sides to this coin.

De-scenting

'De-scenting' a ferret is purely for the sake of its owner and should not be done without a great deal of thought. Ferrets have a pair of glands in the anal canal which can produce a strong musk if the animal is badly upset. In the mating season the hob uses his glands in a minor way when he scent-marks a territory, and all ferret droppings have a slight musky odour from the same glands. The sudden release of a really pungent stink may serve to warn off a predator – weasels and skunks deliberately use their scent glands as defensive weapons. You might feel that it is unwise to deprive a ferret of this means of defence just in case he does escape from your protection, and many veterinary surgeons consider removal of scent glands to be 'mutilation'. You should listen carefully to your vet's advice.

HOME TREATMENT

Some problems can only be dealt with by a vet, but quite often you can take immediate steps at home to alleviate the situation. Whatever the problem, be calm, gentle and firm. An injured animal will be in pain and frightened and a sick animal feels vulnerable and defensive. In both cases reassurance is needed. It may be necessary to restrain the animal but be careful not to cause it extra alarm. If you place it in an unfamiliar situation – perhaps on top of a table instead of on the ground – the novelty might cause uncertainty rather than fear and the ferret might be more cooperative. But take care: a frightened animal is certainly more likely to bite.

If restraint is necessary, do not use a muzzle unless the ferret is used to such a device because you will only make it more apprehensive. Ask someone else to hold it for you, or wrap it in a towel.

It is sensible to keep a basic first-aid kit of items which can easily be obtained without veterinary prescription. Some suggestions for a first-aid box are given below.

Maintenance and First-aid Box

Hospital Savlon disinfectant	Alcohol for tick removal	Cotton buds
Gentian violet	(surgical spirit, paraffin)	Surgical gauze
Wound dusting powder	Antihistamine for stings	Adhesive plaster
Liquid paraffin	Antibiotic ointment	Bandages
Emetic salt	Vaseline	Thermometer
Bicarbonate of soda	Scissors	Medicine dropper
Kaolin or bismuth	Nail-clippers	(unchewable)
'Complan' convalescent diet	Forceps	Feeding-bottle set
Glucose	Wooden spatula	for orphans
Anti-parasite powders	Cottonwool	

Bites

Ferret bites In the breeding season you might have to deal with bites inflicted by hobs on each other during fights, or by a hob on the scruff of a jill's neck during mating. The jill will come in for some rough treatment in the nature of things and occasionally her neck gets sore enough to need attention; she may even develop abscesses. Clip the fur so that you can see where the damage is (if you moisten the fur first, it will stick to the scissors and keep away from the wound). Clean the bitten area gently but thoroughly with water containing salt to counteract infection (2 teaspoons of salt to 1 pint of water). Use an antiseptic like Hospital Savlon or dust with wound-dressing powder, which is less likely to be licked off than an ointment. Licking is in fact probably as good a treatment as any but it is hardly likely that a jill's tongue will be able to reach her own scruff! If it looks bad, go to the vet for antibiotic treatment.

Rat bites These can be very serious and could lead to nasty infections. If you use your ferret for ratting you should be aware of the risks. Make sure you have vaccinated against leptospirosis. Rat bites can in the first place be treated as above for ferret bites, but you are advised to seek veterinary treatment as soon as possible.

Insect bites and stings Clean gently with soap and water, wipe with alcohol such as surgical spirit, and dry. If there is a sting, remove it. Use sodium bicarbonate on a cold wet compress to reduce swelling and itching, or use an antihistamine. An ice pack helps to reduce severe swelling. The most dangerous sting is one that causes swelling at the back of the throat and threatens to impede respiration and feeding – get to the vet quickly.

Snake bites Don't panic! In Britain the only poisonous snake is the adder and ferrets rarely get bitten by one – they are much too smart and can move as quickly as the snake so that if it does strike they probably avoid a lethal dose. Being such small animals a lethal dose is certainly possible, although some people believe that polecats are immune to adder venom. If you *know* that the ferret has been bitten by an adder, keep the animal quiet in its own dark box and get to the vet immediately – which, if you are out in the field, is easier said than done. You could try and apply a tourniquet but it is difficult to do so and the last thing you want is to agitate the ferret.

Convulsions

Convulsions in an animal can be very alarming but they should be allowed to take their course unless they continue for more than five minutes, in which case you need a vet urgently. Be very quiet and calm. Usually convulsions stop of their own accord. They may be caused by certain infections, tetanus, head injuries, brain tumours, parasites, poisoning or drugs, metabolic or congenital abnormalities or – the most likely cause in a ferret – overheating, which is something you can avoid with a bit of commonsense (see Heatstroke).

Diarrhoea

Diarrhoea may be a sign of various diseases or it may simply be caused by what the ferret has eaten. Bread-and-milk diets can produce very loose droppings; so can too much fat, food which is off, a sudden change of diet, or allergy to certain foods. You can take first-aid measures: starve for 24 hours (making sure the ferret has access to plenty of fresh water) and dose with kaolin solution or bismuth. When you start feeding again, do so gradually. But if diarrhoea persists, or has blood or mucus with it, take a sample and your ferret to the vet. Diarrhoea can also be caused by bacteria, constant stress (laboratory animals often have loose droppings), internal parasites, poisoning, tumours and digestive disorders, or it can be indicative of something as serious as distemper, botulism or proliferative colitis, each of which can be fatal and need professional diagnosis and treatment.

Heatstroke

This is a condition which can and should be avoided. Ferrets are very easily overcome by heat and you must always avoid submitting them to heat stress. Take care over the siting of hutches and protect them from the sun. Never leave ferret carriers out in full sun – the confined space can get very warm even in winter sunshine, and don't forget that the sun moves around in the course of a day's ferreting. Be very careful in a vehicle: if you shut your ferrets in the car boot for any length of time they could be in serious trouble.

Ferrets are not efficient at losing excess heat from their bodies. They do not sweat (despite the old name for heatstroke being 'the sweats') and they lose very little heat by panting. They can put up with the cold, but *not* with the heat.

Signs of heatstroke are obvious distress and raised body temperature. The ferret will probably stretch out and seem to be gasping for air. It will very soon collapse and go into a coma; its skin will be hot and dry and its lips pale grey.

It is essential to act fast to get the body temperature down. Immediately remove the animal from the hot environment to a cool, shady, airy situation. Soak its body in cold water and fan it vigorously to help the water's cooling effects. The quickest way of cooling is to ensure that cold air reaches the lungs but that is not easy – water drenching is more practical. If the ferret is conscious, wash its mouth thoroughly in cold water to help the cooling process and let it have small drinks of water. Keep repeating all these cooling techniques until the temperature is reduced, and in the meantime head fast for the vet. Check the ferret's temperature every quarter of an hour and repeat the cooling techniques if it starts to rise again. Normal rectal temperature is quite high – 101.8F on average.

Poisoning

There is a possibility, although it is not very likely, that a working or escaped ferret might eat a poisoned bait or rodent and there is also the unpleasant possibility of deliberate poisoning. The problem is that you and your vet need to identify the poison in order to apply the right anti-dote. The aims of first-aid treatment are to prevent absorption of any more poison into the animal's system, to remove what has already been ingested, to reassure the animal and then to give a specific antidote if there is one.

If the poison is corrosive (acid, alkali, petrol, paraffin etc) do *not* try to induce vomiting. Feed milk or vegetable oil to dilute the poison and get to the vet quickly. For other poisons you can try to induce vomiting by giving hydrogen peroxide orally every five or ten minutes for half an hour (and save the vomit for veterinary evaluation); you can try to dilute the ingested substance by giving lots of water or milk containing medicated charcoal (from the chemist) or kaolin; you can try coating the stomach walls (to prevent internal absorption of the poison) by giving as much milk, veget-able oil, kaolin, bismuth or egg whites as the ferret will willingly take. But if the animal is in an excitable state or in convulsion, do *not* induce vom-iting and do *not* give anything orally – just get to the vet fast, keeping the ferret warm and keeping its head slightly lowered to drain out fluids.

Respiratory troubles

Acute breathing problems are shown by gasping or by slow shallow breath-ing; lips, tongue and inner eyelids may be dark red or bluish. If breath-ing stops and the pupils become dilated, the ferret is in real trouble.

Causes include an obstruction at the back of the throat, or fluid on the lungs. It has been known, for example, for a ferret to get tracheal rings from its food wrapped around the base of its tongue. Open its mouth to check for obstructions; hold its tongue (with a piece of cloth or paper to stop it slipping from your grasp) and pull it forward. Try and hook out the obstruction with your finger (difficult!) or by swabbing with cotton buds.

If the animal has been drowning or has fluid in its throat, hold it upside down by the back quarters (*not* the tail!) for up to half a minute to drain the fluid out of its lungs.

Artificial respiration on a ferret is not easy but you could try the kiss of life through its nostrils or you could try pressing and releasing its ribs carefully if you know what you are doing, for up to an hour.

If there is no heartbeat or pulse, try tapping the chest quite sharply just behind the shoulder.

Shock

Signs of shock include pale mouth, lips and eyelids; rapid and faint pulse; sunken, staring eyes (dilated pupils is a very bad sign); and cool skin from poor blood circulation. General weakness can degenerate into collapse, coma and unconsciousness.

First-aid aims to restore body heat and circulation (by massage), to give adequate fresh air, to keep the ferret warm with blankets and to reassure it. Give small drinks of tepid water with half teaspoonful of salt and half teaspoonful of bicarbonate of soda to a quart of water, and continue to give drinks every half an hour unless it is unconscious, convulsing or vomiting (although ferrets rarely vomit). Quiet, rest and warmth are important while you wait for the vet.

Wounds

Any wounded animal is likely to be frightened, on the defensive and possibly shocked. Reassurance is important.

First stop any bleeding: using a clean handkerchief press it steadily over the wound with the flat of your hand, trying to bring the edges of the wound together as you do so. Then bandage the pad firmly in place. Also apply pressure to any artery which is pumping blood to the wound.

If there is no need to control bleeding, proceed as for Bites (p. 73). You will need to protect the wound from contamination by cleaning it and applying antibiotic and a covering. You might also have to treat for shock, and you will almost certainly need your vet.

NURSING

To take temperature, apply a little vaseline to the bulb of the thermometer and insert it gently into the anus.

To give an oral dose, either grind up pills in a favourite food or in milk if you can be certain that it will all be consumed, or try and slip a small pill in between the teeth at the hinge of the jaw so that by keeping the mouth

closed the ferret is encouraged to swallow before he knows what is happening. Liquid doses are given with a non-chewable dropper.
Injections should only be given under the guidance of your vet.

DISORDERS

Abscesses

Ferrets do seem to develop abscesses, particularly after skin wounds such as bites, or around the jaw and throat from tooth infections or injury by bone fragments. There have also been cases of anal and vaginal abscesses caused by foreign bodies such as hayseeds and barley awns. Treatment of abscesses involves lancing and thorough draining, followed by a course of antibiotics.

Distemper

Canine distemper has always been a major killer of ferrets; they are very susceptible to it unless protected by vaccination. It is a virus and they can catch it from dogs, by direct contact or indirectly through dog urine or through someone who has been handling unvaccinated dogs. Typical signs of distemper are running eyes and gummed-up lids, catarrh, a scabby rash under the chin, lack of appetite, swollen and sore feet, and possibly diarrhoea. If nervous twitches occur you have a very sick ferret; it will probably drool profusely, have convulsions, and finally go into a coma before dying.

Your vet will recognize distemper immediately. It is difficult to treat a stricken ferret and it is exceedingly contagious to other ferrets – you run the risk of losing the lot. A very mild case might recover given careful nursing; it means constant attention, cleaning the eyes and nose frequently, coaxing an unwilling animal to eat, keeping it warm and clean, and making quite sure that it is totally isolated from any unvaccinated ferrets.

Nowadays distemper is much less prevalent, largely because most dogs are vaccinated against it. Be warned that dogs are often vaccinated with a preparation from ferret-cell culture and under no circumstances should such a vaccination be used on a ferret because it will probably *give* it distemper. Details of appropriate vaccinations are given in Vet Check and the first dose should be given at about 6 weeks old.

'Flu

Ferrets and people can catch each other's influenza and common colds quite readily and you should avoid going near your ferret if you are infected. Indeed ferrets have played an important role in helping researchers to understand and combat 'flu in humans. Symptoms in ferrets are much like those in humans: fever, listlessness, lack of appetite and perhaps some sneezing. The illness usually responds to good nursing within a few days and only in rare cases do complications develop.

Paralysis

Paralysis in ferrets is sometimes an inherited disorder which becomes apparent in quite young litters. It may be due to spinal fractures or disk disease. Paralysis of the hind legs can be a sign of the later stages of tuberculosis and sometimes affects all four limbs; it is often accompanied by emaciation. (See 'Vet Check' for other causes of paralysis.)

Skin troubles

Hair loss might make you wonder if something is wrong with your ferret. There is the normal seasonal moulting, and pregnant jills in particular might become alarmingly scruffy and motheaten. Mange is a possibility or there may be dietary causes, like too many eggs.

Ferrets suffer from many of the same external parasites as dogs and cats. They get fleas, lice and mites but these can all be dealt with using appropriate powders, shampoos and veterinary treatment. They quite often get ticks, particularly around the neck and throat if they have been rabbiting. If you find a tick soak it in alcohol (eg surgical spirit or paraffin). It might drop off of its own accord within a few hours, or you might have to pull it off very carefully, making sure that you do not leave its biting parts embedded in the ferret. Ticks do not do much harm and they will drop off anyway once they have gorged themselves, but unless you remove them they will continue their breeding cycle and could become a problem. It is no good simply letting them drop off: if they land on the floor of the hutch or shed the breeding cycle will continue and the very numerous offspring will soon clamber up for another meal of ferret blood. So remove the tick and dust out the hutch itself at regular intervals to destroy any parasites that may be lurking.

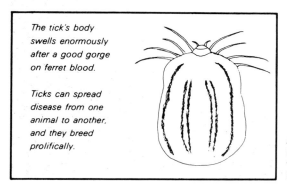

The tick's body swells enormously after a good gorge on ferret blood.

Ticks can spread disease from one animal to another, and they breed prolifically.

Figure 8 Tick. Do not try to pull off a tick which has embedded its mouthparts in a ferret: dab it with petrol or paraffin. A drop of iodine might induce it to let go.

VACCINATION
Ferrets should be vaccinated regularly for protection against canine distemper and leptospirosis. There is some doubt about whether they succumb to any form of parvovirus and it is not common veterinary practice to vaccinate against something unnecessarily. Those who breed ferrets for commercial reasons on a large scale might wish to vaccinate against botulism, and the Fur Breeders Association can give you more information.

JILLS' ILLS
Many a ferret keeper has seen a favourite jill fade away and die, and more often than not it will be a jill which has not been mated during that season. There are several factors involved and more research is still needed, but the fact that jills are 'induced ovulators' is probably at the root of it. As explained in the next chapter, a jill remains in season until she is mated. In confinement she may not have the opportunity of mating and in that case her season can be prolonged for several months. In such a state she is prone to various infections, increasingly so the longer she remains on heat, and it is quite important to terminate her heat early in the season, either by mating or by artificial means.

Pregnant and nursing jills are also considered in the next chapter.

7 Breeding and Litters

Polecats live on their own for much of the year. In spring, however, they come into season. The male's testes grow and the female's vulva becomes considerably swollen and obvious. The male has set up his territory; one or more females, looking for suitable nesting places, may enter that territory. On his own ground the male has exclusive mating rights to the females that have chosen to take up residence. Quite often a female will have some preference for a particular male, especially if she has mated with him in a previous season, but it is debatable whether she selects him for his own sake, or because he is dominant enough to stop other males pestering her, or simply because he has managed to command the area in which she wants to raise her young.

When a male and female meet, they mate. They sniff at each other's scent glands and start chattering excitedly. The male seizes his mate roughly by the scruff of her neck and attempts to drag her, scolding loudly, into a secluded spot. If she slips free there is a chase with a lot of squealing and chattering until he grabs her again. Sooner or later she goes quite limp in his grip and he pulls her into a burrow or the undergrowth, where they mate.

Farmed mink are not much different in their mating behaviour. When they are put together they take a few mutual sniffs and start a very affable 'chuckling'. Very soon the female is racing around the cage with the male in hot pursuit. When she is ready she will let him grab her scruff in his teeth, and he then hauls her into a position under his body, usually throwing her on to her side, and puts his forepaws around her neck. Copulation takes on average half an hour but can last for ten minutes to several hours.

Ferrets, typically of most domesticated animals, usually mate with any other ferret or polecat, although here again a jill may, given the option, prefer a previous mate. Given no choice, almost any mate will do as long as it is the breeding season and as long as she is on heat. Laboratory jills, like farm mink, may well react to stress and persistent breeding by refusing to mate, and although ferret mating sounds and looks like rape the hob will not succeed if the jill does not let him.

Along with many other vertebrate animals living in temperate regions, ferrets are *photoperiodic breeders*. In common with a few species (such as other mustelids, cats, rabbits and some mice) jills are *induced ovulators*. Unlike the closely related stoat, ferrets do not extend their gestation period by *delayed implantation*, whereas the fisher (a marten) extends gestation to eleven months.

Broadly speaking, these facts mean that hobs and jills are only able to breed during a certain season which relates to day-length; that jills will only be receptive to hobs' advances when they themselves are 'on heat' or 'in oestrus' during that season; that without the tactile stimulus of mating a jill will remain constantly on heat until the end of the photoperiodically determined breeding season, but that as soon as she receives the necessary stimulation of mating her ovary releases several ripe eggs which, if male sperm are present, are fertilized and begin to develop in the jill's womb. In order to understand ferret breeding, it is worth taking a closer look at these processes and conditions. The next few paragraphs are a bit technical: if you are only interested in the practical, jump to the section headed Mating.

PHOTOPERIODISM
Photoperiodism is the response of an organism to the relative length of periods of darkness and light. In photoperiodic breeders the timing of the mating season is governed by the average length (and possibly intensity and wavelength) of continuous daylight, or, some people argue, the length of continuous darkness between periods of light of whatever length. Photoperiodism in mammals is effective through the pituitary gland, which lies beneath the 'floor' of the brain and which is stimulated to secrete hormones which in turn stimulate the growth of ovarian follicles and oocytes in the female ovary and the formation of spermatazoa in male testes.

In the ferret it seems that the male responds to a short day-length. Very soon after the shortest day in the natural year his testes, which have almost disappeared from sight since autumn, begin to drop down again into the scrotum and gradually enlarge. They are fully developed two or three months later and are soon able to produce viable sperm. The hob remains in breeding condition for another four or five months and then his testes begin to reduce and disappear again up into his body cavity. Thus the hob is ready to breed from early spring and through much of the summer. He is at his most fertile in late spring and early summer.

The jill, however, responds to long day-length and seems to require an average of at least fourteen hours of uninterrupted day light in any 24-hour period before she can become responsive for breeding. The subject of photoperiodism in the ferret, we should warn you, is still far from comprehensively understood, despite many years of research, and the situation is not straightforward. The Bibliography (p. 179) mentions several scientific investigations into the intricacies, which need only concern you if you are involved in large-scale commercial breeding. It is possible to control breeding seasons by using artificial lighting that gives a continuous optimum day-length so that jills are always receptive and able to breed. It is possible to overdo it: too much daylight can inhibit reproduction. Sheffield University and Dr John Hammond Jr of Cambridge, among others, have been able to manipulate day-length so that jills can produce several litters a year, at any time of year, but there are physiological as well as moral limitations to such exploitive breeding schedules.

Once the longer day-lengths have triggered the jill's pituitary gland, she becomes in oestrus or on heat (there is, literally, a noticeable increase in her body temperature) and will remain so until oestrus is terminated either by mating (or simulated mating), by hormonal treatment, or by the ending of the breeding season because of shortening day-length.

Some mammals have oestrus cycles – they will be on heat for, say, a few days then off, then on again and so on. Jills, however, are polyoestrous: once they are on heat the state is continuous until it is terminated as just explained. The jill's potential season starts and ends later than the average hob's; she could in theory still breed as late as early autumn, perhaps a couple of months after the hob's testes have ceased to produce viable sperm. While she is in oestrus, her vulva is visibly very swollen.

The chart shows how the male and female potential breeding seasons overlap. It is only during the overlap period that mating can occur: the jill will not accept the hob's advances unless she is in oestrus. Note also that at either end of the seasons fertility in both sexes is increased or reduced gradually. To ensure breeding success it is important to choose a time when fertility is at a high level in male *and* female.

INDUCED OVULATION

Many animals are 'spontaneous ovulators', ie the female's ovary releases ripe eggs regardless of whether or not mating has occurred. If sperm are introduced while the ripe egg is still viable, fertilization can take place, but more often than not mating will be too late or too early for the egg.

Mammals that normally live rather solitary lives tend to be 'induced ovulators': they need specific stimuli to release ripe eggs. The advantage of induced ovulation is that at *every* mating sperm and ova are likely to meet and less likely to be wasted. The more or less continuous state of the female's sexual readiness during the season enables full advantage to be taken on the relatively rare occasions when male and female come across each other.

In some birds the stimuli for induced ovulation might be visual displays or making the right noises. In some mammals certain odours will be the trigger. In ferrets the jill seems to require physical stimulation in order to

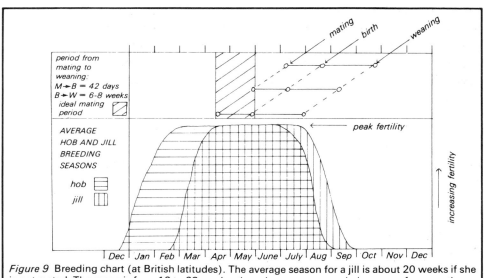

Figure 9 Breeding chart (at British latitudes). The average season for a jill is about 20 weeks if she is not mated. The range is from 12 to 28 weeks, though some can remain in season for more than 30 weeks.

ovulate, but odour (pheromones) might also be a factor. The general consensus is that ovulation in the jill is induced by cervical and vaginal stimulation, but there are other theories that place the emphasis on other aspects in the courtship routine. It is possible that biting and gripping the back of the jill's neck and dragging her around are as important as actual copulation in inducing ovulation. If ferret AI ever becomes standard practice, this factor should perhaps be borne in mind!

There are also reports which seem to indicate that the smell of a hob might be enough on its own to induce ovulation in certain circumstances, the implication being that his actual physical presence is unnecessary – although of course there will be no litter if the eggs are not fertilized with sperm. In such circumstances the jill becomes *pseudopregnant*: she will not thereafter accept any sexual advances from the hob and she goes through all the same physiological and behavioural changes as a genuinely pregnant jill, for the same length of gestation, but of course she does not give birth at the end of it all. She may well be able to help another jill look after her kits, and will often be quite determined to do so.

To summarize briefly thus far:

1 The hob is stimulated by short day-length to come into breeding condition from early spring to mid-summer. His testes descend into the scrotum and are enlarged during that period.

2 The jill is triggered by long day-length to come into oestrus and her

vulva becomes noticeably swollen and exposed. Only when in oestrus will she accept sexual approaches by a hob.

3 The jill remains in oestrus until stimulated to ovulate either by direct cervical and vaginal stimulation and/or possibly in response to other aspects of courtship behaviour and/or pheromones.

4 If ovulation is induced by copulation with a fertile male, the jill normally becomes pregnant; in other circumstances she becomes pseudopregnant.

5 In the absence of induced ovulation the jill remains in oestrus until the end of the breeding season. Her vulval swelling will reduce after ovulation has been induced or when the breeding season ends.

MATING

The ferret breeding season begins when the female is ready to accept the male, usually in late spring. She can remain on heat for the entire summer but it is better from all points of view to mate her quite early in the season. Polecats breed in spring so that the young, born six weeks after mating, arrive when food is abundant, the weather kind and they have plenty of time to grow, harden and become independent before the going gets tougher.

With domesticated ferrets, early mating is for slightly different reasons. Firstly, the health of the jill is likely to suffer if she remains on heat for too long, secondly the hob will become sterile before the end of the jill's season, and thirdly hot weather later in the year can not only inhibit breeding but can also cause considerable problems in giving birth and nursing the litter. On the other hand, breeding should not be attempted until the male's testicles are fully developed and able to produce viable sperm, and the female's vulva is fully swollen. April/May is a good time to breed your ferrets in Britain.

The onset of the jill's heat is easily recognized. Her vulva swells up to as much as fifty times its usual size, and is pink and exposed. Full breeding size is reached a fortnight or so after the initial swelling is first noticeable. She sometimes secretes fluid, often enough to dampen her thighs and the underside of her tail, and you might also notice an increase in her body musk. Her behaviour might alter subtly – she may sprawl on her belly in an almost provocative manner. She will also shed hair, but will not moult properly until she has ovulated.

The hob's readiness to breed is also obvious. His testes move back towards the anus and become more prominent and turgid, and almost naked (during winter his scrotum has been partly hidden by his winter coat and has become soft and small because the testes have moved up into his body cavity). His odour certainly increases in the season and he be-

When the jill is in oestrus and ready to mate her vulva is noticeably swollen.
Normally it is unobtrusive.

comes generally more aggressive – to men as well as to other hobs. He
might try and start mating before the jill is in oestrus. She will not allow
him to do so but if she is unable to escape his attentions he will persist in
grabbing her scruff and trying to mount her, giving her a sore neck and
sore temper. To save aggravation and possible injury, it is best to separate
him from other ferrets, male or female. However well they know each
other, two hobs are likely to argue, if not fight, in the breeding season, and
if they are in a confined area where there is no possibility of a dignified
retreat they can really damage each other. You might be lucky and never
have as much as a raised eyebrow between them but be aware of the
possibility of trouble.

A vasectomized hob has only been deprived of the means of unloading
sperm from his testes to his penis. In every other respect he is thoroughly
male and will have exactly the same instincts as any other, fertile, hob; so
he, too, must be isolated for the sake of peace.

Hobbles (castrated males) usually cause fewer problems, but some of
them, like castrated dogs, will persist in mounting and causing general
aggravation and might even persist in scruff-biting to such an extent that
any companions risk very raw necks, in which case hobbles must also be
separated.

On-heat jills can often be left together for a while, but they too may
begin bullying each other if they remain in oestrus for too long. They can

also occasionally induce ovulation in each other, which gives you pseudo-pregnant jills, so if you want to breed from your jills either do so early in the season or separate them.

In the wild, the polecat male holds the territory and a female in breeding condition meets him on his own ground. With farm mink it makes very little difference whether the male is brought to the female or vice versa. With ferrets, some people prefer to take the hob to the jill, but often they are already sharing accommodation anyway and are just left to get on with it in their own time.

Ferret mating is just as rough and raucous as that of wild polecats. Anxious keepers should not interfere, however violent it sounds. Let the pair get on with it in privacy, and give them plenty of time together: it can take anything from five minutes to half an hour for the hob to achieve entry, and then they may stay locked together for three or four hours. Leave them together at least a couple of days so that they can repeat the performance. The skin on the jill's neck is often broken by the hob's teeth; if you leave them together for more than about a week she could get a very sore neck indeed so the hob should be removed.

Weather conditions play a part in breeding success. The male's scrotum serves to keep the testes a couple of degrees cooler than his usual body temperature and this is important for fertility. Old shepherds knew a trick or two: if a ram's testes were bound against his underbelly so that they were kept warm, the ram would become temporarily sterile. If a hob's testes are too warm he also becomes sterile, and if the jill becomes over-heated so that her body temperature is too high the fertilized eggs will not implant in the uterus. If the eggs are already fertilized and implanted, heat can damage the brain and nerve cells of the embryo and the kit could be born half the normal size or with deformities like hydrocephalus or a cleft palate. And if the accommodation is too warm when the kits are born there are several increasingly unpleasant possibilities: the jill may fail to chew through the umbilical cords; she may fail to produce milk so that the kits starve; the kits might die in the womb because she fails to give birth with the result that the placenta stops growing but the young continue to grow in the womb and are asphyxiated by the restrictive placenta. At daytime temperatures of 85F ferrets can mate but the jill will probably not become pregnant, although as long as it cools down at night she will probably thrive in herself. But at a constant 70F day *and* night the pair are unlikely to breed at all.

UNMATED JILLS

If a jill is not given the opportunity to mate, she will remain on heat for the rest of the breeding season in a condition known as prolonged or persistent oestrus. Her vulva stays swollen for several months and can become dry and sore, in which case you can apply a soothing lubricant. But be warned that the longer she remains in an oestral state the more vulnerable she becomes to infection. The vulva itself is very exposed and infection can find its way into the vagina and uterus. If she is then mated, the uterine secretions become a perfect medium for the developing eggs – and for bacteria. You may well have a very sick jill ten or fourteen days after mating, with a discharge of pus from an infected womb. She could then develop a generalized infection and peritonitis and you might lose her. On the other hand, the infection sometimes seems to clear of its own accord but in fact it persists down in the uterine glands and will blow up again next time she is mated.

A jill that remains in oestrus for any length of time (bearing in mind that the wild animal would mate at the first opportunity) can become seriously ill. You might be lucky and get her through the whole season without any apparent trouble, year after year, but it is not a risk worth taking. Old ferreters were convinced that an unmated jill was bound to fade away and die in her second season, and they were not necessarily wrong even if sometimes they were too hasty in their diagnosis and knocked the old lady on the head too soon.

Any jill, however fit, will lose a lot of weight and a lot of fur during the breeding season but this is not a sign of illness. However, there is a substantial risk that a jill staying on heat for too long will develop all sorts of problems, the least of which is a sore vulva or an infected womb. She tends to lose far more weight than she should and gradually becomes weaker. Many unmated jills succumb to bone marrow disease, which is often fatal and is thought to affect up to fifty per cent of jills who are not brought out of oestrus one way or another during the season. The disease is probably encouraged by the continuously high levels of oestrogen produced in the unmated oestrus jill and she will lose her appetite and become depressed, dehydrated and anaemic (look for less-than-pink pads, gums and inner eyelids). She may show signs of fever and if these are followed by a sudden and dramatic drop in body temperature, death is imminent.

Bone marrow disease is discussed in more detail in the Vet Check section in Part II. It is very difficult to treat, particularly as it is usually too late by the time you realize that your jill is really ill. Your vet might be able to save her with a course of antibiotics, force feeding, blood transfusions and emergency surgery (hysterectomy) if she is strong enough to stand the anaesthetic, but it will be an expensive and lengthy business needing months of careful nursing. The best treatment is prevention – and prevention means mating early in the season, or spaying if you will never want to breed from the jill, or asking your vet for hormonal treatment (the 'jill pill' or 'jill jab' discussed in Vet Check) which should be given right at the beginning of the season. An alternative is to use a vasectomized hob to bring her out of oestrus without making her pregnant, and some clubs might share such a hob. If they do, it is important to take precautions against spreading any kind of disease, whether genital or general.

PSEUDOPREGNANCY

Very early in the season a hob will be sexually active but will not be able to produce enough viable sperm so that if he is allowed to mate he will perform as he should, inducing the jill to ovulate and come out of oestrus, but her eggs will not be fertilized. She will then go through all the physiological and behavioural changes associated with pregnancy – even to the extent of swollen belly and teats – but it is a false pregnancy and at the end of the normal gestation period (42 days – or a day or two later in pseudopregnancy) she will act as if she has given birth. It will, of course, be a phantom litter existing only in her imagination and she will devote a lot of energy to 'nursing' any substitute she can find, even trying to drag a large and protesting hob into her nest by the scruff of his neck as if he was a mere kit.

You might think that this is a possible method of overcoming the problems of prolonged oestrus but it is a haphazard one – she might reject the hob anyway, or she might become genuinely pregnant. A successfully vasectomized hob is the safer bet.

Pseudopregnancy can result from implantation failure due to reduced light intensity a month before mating, and in late summer the reducing hours of daylight can have the same effect so if you want to breed late use electric lighting to extend 'daylight' hours artificially. At the beginning of the season mink farmers, who have a commercial incentive for successful breeding, measure the male animal's testicles during February (mink mate earlier than ferrets and their mating period is restricted to four weeks in the year) and will not put him anywhere near a female unless his testicles are judged to be of a good size, because fertility seems to increase with size.

Pseudopregnancy sometimes arises from sexual activity between frustrated jills housed together when they are on heat. We have heard of a case where a recently mated jill was caged with an unmated jill and the latter spontaneously ovulated in response, apparently, to the smell of the hob on the mated jill. Some ferreters put a hob-scented brick in an unmated jill's cage with the same result but, again, this is a hit-and-miss method of trying to induce ovulation and bring the jill out of oestrus. It is better to mate her properly and breed from her, or to spay her, or to go and talk to your vet about hormonal treatment. Some vets will offer reduced rates to clubs because they can treat several jills at the same time.

SUCCESSFUL MATING

There are several ways of telling whether or not mating has successfully induced ovulation (although that does not necessarily mean the jill is genuinely pregnant). The mated female will moult into a shorter coat. Her swollen vulva will become dry instead of moist, perhaps three days after mating if it is early in the season, and will then begin to reduce to its original inconspicuous size. The rate of reduction depends on how long she has been on heat: if it is early in the season the shrinking takes less time than the swelling, but later in the season the vulva will only reduce slowly. If she is not mated at all the vulva reduces at the end of the breeding season by shrivelling quite quickly.

At perhaps three weeks after mating your vet will be able to 'palpate', ie feel the young in the womb. Some jills hardly show any swelling of the pregnant belly at all and you could find it difficult to detect whether or not she has any young in there. She could surprise you and produce a dozen!

PREGNANCY

The gestation period is six weeks (42 days), give or take a day or two. The wild polecat during this time will prepare a private nursery for her litter and she will not tolerate the presence of the hob or other jills near the time of the birth. The nursery is usually deep into her burrow in a special nesting chamber at the end of a tunnel. She forms her bedding into a spherical nest with one small opening, and the young stay within its confines for the first two or three weeks. The litter normally numbers up to a dozen at birth but only four to eight kits survive to the weaning stage. They are smaller than a man's thumb when they are born; they weigh about a third of an ounce; and they are deaf, blind, pink, almost naked and vociferous. Their loud squeaking often catches the ear of a curious predator such as a fox, but predators are no match for an angry polecat mother.

Polekits' eyes do not open fully until they are five weeks old but they begin to wander about the burrow at about three weeks, while they are still blind. At this stage they will eat prey brought in by the mother, as well as suckling her milk, and they are careful to use a communal latrine in the tunnels so that the nest itself is kept clean. The mother is constantly dragging them back into the nest, with a lot of chattering and scolding, but, like any ferret, they always want to be somewhere other than where they are and she has a full-time job retrieving them to the safety of the chamber. They are always on the move and chuntering to each other.

When their eyes are open all their senses are alert; they become very playful and begin to react quickly to any unusual sound, sight or smell, but the mother still tries to drag them back underground whenever they stray. By about eight weeks old they have been fully weaned off milk and are ready to learn about hunting, setting off in Indian file behind their protective mother. The family stays together until the young are perhaps three months old, when they begin to break up into small playful groups, but they gradually drift apart to live the solitary lives of adult polecats.

If the female polecat has successfully reared a first litter she is unlikely to produce a second one in the same year, although she will probably come on heat again once the young have been weaned, but if she loses her first litter she often does mate again and may produce a second litter even as late as mid-summer.

Like her wild sister, the pregnant ferret will seek out a private nursery for her coming litter and will build a good warm nest in a dark secluded place. Give her access to an enclosed nestbox with a small pophole entrance; make sure that the kits cannot fall out accidentally or they may run the risk of hypothermia if she fails to drag them back in again in the early days of their lives. Avoid drafty open-topped boxes and do not use metal floors: wood is much warmer. Provide adequate ventilation and good insulation. There should be at least eight inches of straw or four inches of wood shavings for the bedding: let the jill help herself to as much bedding as she wants.

The jill will feel more at ease in a familiar environment and as you want to avoid all possible stress it is important to give her plenty of time to get used to a nesting hutch if it is not her usual home. She needs to feel that it is her own, so she should have it to herself for at least two weeks before giving birth. If the hob has stayed with her after mating, remove him as soon as she seems to get restless and starts nest-making.

If she is used to the company of other ferrets, let her withdraw gradually into this new privacy. Mated females might or might not argue if housed together. A jill should be confined alone with her young until they are weaned at about six to eight weeks old and, bearing in mind how fast they grow, you should ensure that the nesting hutch can accommodate them.

In a communal housing system, ensure that each pregnant jill has her own nesting box (let her choose which one). In the early life of the litter unusual disturbance of any kind may induce a jill to kill her young, but a little later on she will be quite happy to share her maternal duties with a familiar 'aunty'.

During her pregnancy the jill's vulva will gradually reduce its swelling. She begins to lose her winter coat, often dramatically and to such an extent that she goes almost bald in patches before her new short coat grows through. Without the winter fur she can look too thin for comfort, but her appetite increases and you should give her as much food as she wants so that she can build up her reserves. Then she will have something to draw on when she is suckling the kits.

Pregnancy, giving birth and nursing the kits all place substantial demands on the jill and she needs to be fit enough to cope. Do not overfeed her before breeding – you want her to be fit, not fat, and adequate protein is much more important than carbohydrates. Include a dash of salt in her diet from early summer onwards against the possibility of 'nursing sickness'. During breeding, pregnancy and nursing you must ensure that she receives adequate (but not excessive) vitamin E; a deficiency can result in infertility, abortion, resorption of the foetus, anaemia, lack of milk and starvation of the litter. Good sources of vitamin E are vegetable oils and eggs but the best insurance is to include raw liver in her diet (up to about ten per cent of her total ration). Go easy on eggs – they can lead to loss of coat. Build up her calcium intake gradually (she will lose calcium when she is giving milk) by including fresh bone or bonemeal in the diet. If you normally give her some milk, you can increase the milk ration just a little. Fresh drinking-water must always be available, even more so during nursing. Avoid giving her a poultry-rich diet during pregnancy.

The pregnant jill will probably spend more time sleeping than usual and often becomes exceptionally affectionate towards her keeper. She spends a lot of time in the nest and a few days before the birth she begins to build it up in readiness. Once she has made her nest, be prepared to leave it untouched for several weeks, until the kits have moved out of it. The bedding should *not* be shredded paper or hay: hay is too warm, and shredded paper can entangle kits. Use clean fresh wheat straw.

Signs of imminent birth usually include enlarged nipples, with a little discharge a day before the kits are born. The jill might look a little dreamy; she might pay attention to her vulva when the kits are due, but by this stage she will by choice avoid prying eyes by retiring to the security of the nest.

BIRTH
Most multiple-birth mammals have little problem in actually giving birth: the young are very small and usually come out easily and in quick succes-

sion. The jill is secretive about the process and you should not intrude on her privacy, however well you know her. She *might* not resent you but in the majority of cases your curiosity will cause her acute distress and may lead to the loss of the litter. She has a highly developed alarm system in this respect and will probably kill them if a 'predator' detects their hiding place. (Like it or not, she might regard you as a predator, however much she normally trusts you.)

An inexperienced jill could become confused about the whole business. She might rush to her latrine corner instead of giving birth in the nest. She might even eat them one by one as they emerge. Or she might simply drop them wherever she happens to be and then ignore them but, with maternal instincts in full flood, will try and drag you or a fellow ferret into the nest while her real kits are neglected and left to die. If you interfere, it could even make matters worse!

Next time around she will know better. In the normal birth all the kits usually emerge a few minutes apart but there is sometimes a delay of several hours if the mother has been upset in some way. For example, if you keep her hutch in an open-fronted shed, a familiar but inquisitive animal such as a dog or farm livestock can alarm her so much that she withholds the rest of the litter until the next day. In the meantime she fails to produce milk for those that have already been born and they will die.

Very occasionally a jill might have problems giving birth and all you can really do is make sure she is warm, give her a drink of warm milk containing glucose (so that she gets calcium and carbohydrates) and ask your vet's advice as soon as possible.

Do not be alarmed by this catalogue of dire possibilities – most births are straightforward. If all goes well, she licks at the birth membranes on each kit so that it can breathe, and within minutes the kit begins to squeak. That squeaking and squealing will be your first sign that the litter has arrived and from then on it will be a fairly constant summons for maternal help. The mother remains in the nest and will probably not emerge to eat her food on the first day, but she will eat the afterbirth and that will mean that her droppings will be a black tarry mess. The kits may not suckle immediately but should do so within the first few hours to ensure that they receive important antibodies.

Eating the placenta and navel cord is part of the new mother's routine behaviour, but if it is too warm in the hutch she might fail to eat the cords which could dry up and entangle the kits. If that happens they need your help before they die in a heap, but it is only likely in very hot conditions.

THE LITTER

Jills may produce anything from two to fourteen or more young but the average is usually about eight or nine. At first they are identical to polecat kits – pink and naked except for a fine white fuzz, ears and eyes sealed. Their heads seem to be too large for their bodies and too heavy for them to move easily, but the body catches up after a couple of weeks. By ten days or so they have quite a good covering of white fur (whatever their final colour is going to be) and are becoming active enough to cause their mother considerable exasperation as she is continually retrieving them back into the nest. At about three weeks they begin to sample solid food, although their eyes are still closed so that they rely entirely on smell. Their milk teeth are needle-sharp and your finger is just another potential meal to be tested. If your jill is a pet, she will probably let you begin to handle her young as early as seven days old but in most cases it is wisest to wait until the kits are coming out of the nest regularly. For the first few weeks their mother stays with them in the nest, emerging only to eat and to defecate.

At about three or four weeks old the kits' eyes begin to open and by four to five weeks they are suddenly much prettier altogether: they are as woolly and appealing as any other young animal. With their eyes fully open by five weeks they become very lively and by six weeks they are playing together with plenty of energy and a lot of chatter. Non-albino coats will gradually darken. By nine weeks old the young have already reached half their adult weight.

While she is with her litter, the jill's metabolic rate is particularly high. Not only is she producing milk but she is also under constant stress. Even in the familiar safety of her domestic environment she is instinctively on the alert for predators and she is unflagging in her efforts to keep her young in the nest, dragging them back by the scruff of the neck or even taking most of the body into her mouth. As they grow and become more active her retrieval task is an endless one.

The instinct of any ferret is to go for the back of the neck of anything that moves. Kits have apocrine glands on their necks that make them smell like babies, not food, when their mother grabs them by the scruff! It is just possible that mistakes can be made, particularly by a first-time mother, and occasionally kits are killed. Cannibalism is not unknown, particularly if a hob is left with the family, and it seems to be more common in a large litter (up to sixteen kits is a lot for any mother, especially as she only has eight nipples) and may be a process of natural selection. Sometimes it seems to be an inherited trait and it is possible that in such cases the apocrine glands are not well developed in certain families. If the hob is present the entire litter may be destroyed, otherwise the jill is unlikely to kill more than two or three. And, naturally, what is killed is eaten: there is no point in wasting good protein. Rabbits also commonly re-ingest their young, and rats will eat theirs for the sake of moisture in a dry spell. Make sure your jill has access to plenty of fresh water!

Large litters can also suffer from starvation because there is simply not enough milk to go round, and it is only fair to the jill to take some of the kits off her and give them to a foster mother. Most jills are quite happy to foster if their own litters are small in number, but to encourage acceptance it is worth distracting the foster mother with a good meal while you slip the foundlings in among her own kits so that they all smell the same when she returns to the nest.

However, be wary of causing distress to any jill with a litter because she may well reject all her kits, either by ignoring them or, more likely, by killing them as a natural response to discovery of the nest by a potential predator. The mother has invested a lot of her own nutrients and energy into the litter and rather than let a predator have the benefit of all that goodness, she will take it for herself.

An 'aunty' can be a great help to the nursing jill. One of the jill's usual hutch-mates will happily share the work of retrieving kits back into the nest. Mother and aunt will probably treat each other like kits and try and drag each other back to safety as well, sometimes in mid-meal, but on the whole even that kind of cheek does not seem to cause much aggravation. The kits will 'suckle' aunty – no milk, of course, but she can act as a dummy, and the mother is relieved rather than jealous. Naturally jills vary: some mothers will not tolerate the presence of another jill, however helpful, and some jills will not relish the aunty role, but the mothering instinct is often very strong, particularly if a jill has been pseudopregnant. Some will mother any ferret any time, large or small (and 'small' can be fully adult) and some will also try and drag a familiar human into the nest by the scruff of the wrist or with a firm but gentle grip between your thumb and forefinger.

FEEDING

The nursing jill will need good feeding to replenish her reserves. Be careful not to overfeed her during the first two days after the birth or she could develop udder congestion, but thereafter give her all she wants. Include a calcium supplement (eg milk or bonemeal) to counterbalance the loss of calcium from her body into her milk. She should have at least 6 per cent fresh bone in her diet. Lack of calcium can lead to milk fever, especially in a first-time mother three or four weeks after giving birth; its signs are

Ferret kits of various ages. The youngest kits here are 2 weeks old and their eyes are sealed. As they grow their fur thickens and non-albino kits begin to change colour. The eyes open gradually from about 3 or 4 weeks and are usually fully opened by 5 weeks or so. The final picture in this series shows (from left to right): a year-old hob, a 10-week-old jill and a 5-week-old jill.

Kits begin to take an interest in raw meat at three weeks old, when their eyes are still sealed and eating can be a messy business. A full stomach demands a good snooze. Older kits can deal with a whole young rabbit.

alarming (progressive partial paralysis, tremors and convulsions) and veterinary treatment must be immediate.

Avoid giving the nursing jill too much poultry and make sure she has a daily ration of liver. Peak nursing time is two to four weeks after the birth, and for that period she will need as much good food as you can give her.

The young begin to take an interest in food other than milk from about three weeks old, when they begin to venture out of the nest even though their eyes are still closed. This is an ideal time to start handling them and getting them used to the smell of your fist before their teeth can do you any damage. (Milk teeth begin to erupt at about two weeks old and proper canines develop at six to seven weeks old.) Get the kits used to your voice as well – give a familiar call or whistle as you approach the hutch at feeding time.

At this early stage the feeding youngsters are not a pretty sight! They get themselves plastered with meat-blood; they get right into a bowl of supplementary milk or anything else you give them. They quickly learn to recognize your approach, or to anticipate it if your routines are regular, and they start squeaking and rushing out of the nest all in a body, homing in on the food at full speed and with deadly accuracy even if they are still blind. They may not be strong enough of jaw to chew on whole carcases but they will happily suck on something like lights and their teeth are sharp enough to tackle puppy food and freshly minced raw meat with a little beaten egg. In no time at all they are ready for the same food as their mother. Encourage them on to solid food so that they are not such a drain on the jill. She will usually wean them by six to eight weeks old and you can help by taking them off her one by one, largest first. Now you can clean out the nest thoroughly and give her a fresh start.

Once she has dried up her milk she often comes on heat a week or two later. If it is not too late in the season, you can mate her again, but she will be fairly thin and run down after several weeks of nursing and it is more considerate to give her a well-earned break.

KIT MORTALITY

If every polecat kit in the average litter survived, the countryside would soon be pelting with polecats. The same goes for ferrets, and doubly so as they often do have two litters in the season. However, in the nature of things mortality rates in kits are fairly high and we have already mentioned a few pre-natal and post-natal problems. If you want to make the most of a litter, watch out for the following.

Hypothermia can result from low night temperatures, insufficient nesting material or drafty quarters. An ideal hutch environment is a temperature between 42F and 68F, with good ventilation. If the jill fails to drag a stray kit back into her nest, especially one she dropped casually at birth, it can die quite quickly. Sometimes she will ignore such a newborn kit because it seems to be cold, motionless and dead. However, if you hold the little creature in the warmth of your hand or put it in a warm box with a well-padded hot-water-bottle, more often than not it will soon be breathing, squeaking and wriggling. A few drops of a 10 per cent glucose solution by mouth will help once it is able to take them. As soon as it is warm and vigorous, you can carefully replace it in the nest with the rest of the litter or put it to a foster mother.

Milk failure will lead to starvation during the first three weeks of life. You can discreetly try to observe the jill and see that her young are suckling properly, especially if it is her first litter. Signs of trouble are lethargy in very young kits, or older kits squealing with hunger (there is a much sharper and more urgent pitch to the squeal of a seriously hungry kit). Milk failure may be either an inability to produce milk or a blockage or damaged teats. To avoid the first problem, the jill must have access to plenty of drinking-water (make sure the drinking devices are working properly) and should be given an appropriately supplemented diet and plenty of food. During the second to fifth weeks of lactation watch out for mastitis: the glands will be hard and swollen and the milk may be discoloured or clotted, and there could be an abscess or two which will need lancing. After three weeks of age, when the kits begin to take a little solid food, they will also begin to drink (and paddle in) supplementary milk from a bowl, and this additional milk will reduce the strain on the mother. But teat damage can still be caused by overzealous kits if they are not getting enough solid food as they grow, especially if there are more than eight of them. Some breeders automatically cull the litter to five from the start.

At weaning time watch out for *bloat* in kits – distended stomachs half an hour to four hours after feeding. This is a sign of bad management and can be avoided by practising strict hygiene, making sure the kits are never hungry enough to need to overeat when they are fed (feed at least twice a day and make sure that any runts are getting enough), and making any diet changes only gradually. If you decide to feed cereals (which are not strictly necessary), introduce them very gradually indeed, little by little.

COMMUNE KITS
Some people successfully rear litters in the commune system, where all their ferrets, whatever age or sex, live together most of the time. Nesting boxes are provided but not restricted and if the commune members are

Commune kits – the focus of attention.

used to each other the kits can thrive and become integrated into the enlarged family. It would be sensible to remove uncastrated hobs from the commune just in case, but hobbles can be popular uncles if they are by nature good-tempered. As jills are usually so much smaller than hobs, you can make the nesting-box popholes too small for the hobs to have access.

WEANED KITS

Provided you can give them the space, the litter can stay together for as long as you like, although if the jill is producing a second litter in the same year she will need separate quarters. If you are disposing of some of the litter they will be ready to go from about nine or ten weeks old, preferably twelve weeks. While they remain together they will give a great deal of entertainment, especially given space to exercise and explore. It is a non-stop romp, lots of chattering, helter-skelter dancing and prancing, mock attacks and scraps and general *joie de vivre* – a frolic of ferrets, just like a pother of polecats.

ORPHANS

It is possible, although difficult and time-consuming, to raise orphaned kits or rejected runts by hand if there is no foster jill able to do the job for you. The major keys to whatever success might be possible in hand-rearing – and be warned that success is hard to come by although immensely worthwhile if you can achieve it – are consistency, warmth, hygiene and patience.

Ferret milk has a higher fat content than that of cows, cats and goats (see Table C in Part II). Not surprisingly, no manufacturer has tried to formulate a milk substitute specially for ferret kits, nor have we been able to trace an up-to-date analysis of ferret milk (Table C is based on a 1962 publication).

Rather than try to enrich cow's top-of-the-milk with eggs, it is better to use a consistent source of prepared products suitable for kittens and puppies. It is essential to be consistent in the type of food, the temperature and times at which it is fed, and the warmth of the environment. Practise scrupulous hygiene with everything used in the preparation of the feed. All equipment must be thoroughly cleaned and sterilized before each session: wash in soapy water, rinse completely and then soak in the type of solution used for babies' bottles. Avoid using a tea towel to dry the equipment; either let it dry naturally in fresh air or use clean paper towels every time. Make sure your hands are also well scrubbed.

Young animals are very vulnerable to infection and if you have taken on kits orphaned at birth your problems are substantial because they have not had time to acquire an armour of natural immunities from their mother. Most nursing mammals produce colostrum for at least the first 24 hours after the birth, and colostrum is vital to the newborn animal's immunity system. Any dairy farmer knows how important colostrum is to the young calf and also how the very fact of suckling its own mother and being licked by her seems to increase the calf's resistance to disease. If your kits are being bottlefed only because their mother's milk supply has failed, they can still get antibodies, warmth and bladder stimulation from her, but if she has died you have to give the kits a lot more than milk substitute. You could ask your vet about antibiotics if really necessary, but heed his advice: antibiotics should not be given lightly.

A warm clean nestbox is essential. Use a high-sided basket or cardboard box, or a plastic washing-up bowl if nothing else is available. Insulate it with lots of newspaper, which is warm, absorbent and disposable. Add some bedding – clean straw is best, or perhaps some soft hay or towels but make sure the kits cannot be smothered accidentally; they are very tiny. Place the nestbox in a quiet, warm, dark corner free from draughts – not on the floor – and see that the kits' backs are protected either with good bedding or by fixing a removable lid with plenty of breathing space and airholes. Keep the temperature consistently around 80F for the first two weeks, with about 50–60 per cent humidity. Clean the box out frequently. Better still, have a fresh box ready at feeding time so that you can transfer each kit after it has been fed. That way you will be able to remember which ones *have* been fed, and you can deal with the soiled box later.

Be warned that for at least the first week or two you will have to feed every two hours, *day and night* – or at least ten times in 24 hours. If you are feeding several kits, it will be almost a full-time job. Be prepared, too, for failure. You are taking on a difficult job in the face of the odds.

Preparing the feed

Most pet shops sell suitable feeding bottles: get the smallest possible (Catac's Foster Feeding Bottle Kit is useful). It is possible to adapt a doll's feeding bottle, but such toys do not have proper air inlets and suckling will create a vacuum unless you make a tiny hole at the end of the bottle furthest from the teat. You could use a medicine dropper or pipette in an emergency but the kits are likely to suck in too much air, which gives them wind. (A drop of baby's gripe water on the tongue might bring relief.)

Although it is possible to feed milk at room temperature (as long as you *always* feed it at that temperature) it is much more palatable and digestible fed warm. Keep it at about blood heat and feed it at a consistent temperature – the same temperature at every feed. Once you have mixed the feed, therefore, you will need a warm-water bath. It is difficult to keep small amounts warm and although it seems wasteful it is better to mix up too much, which will stay warm longer. But do not be tempted to save up leftovers for the next feed: you must mix a fresh batch every time.

Equipment for hand rearing orphans.

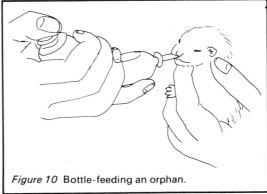

Figure 10 Bottle-feeding an orphan.

The feed

People have tried various milk substitutes for ferret orphans. Hoechst UK Ltd make two useful ones: Cimicat, for kittens, and Welpi, for puppies. Unfortunately none of the manufacturers can give absolute guidelines for ferrets and you need to experiment a little to find the right mixture. Start by following the printed instructions carefully, and adjust gradually if necessary.

How much?

The aim is to feed until the kit shows signs of refusing, then stop! Do not overfeed; if anything, underfeed. Something like ten per cent of body-weight gives you a very rough guideline. If you see signs of diarrhoea, you are overfeeding either in strength of mixture or in quantity of total liquid intake. Check for a steady daily weight gain to ensure you are feeding enough, but expect a *loss* of weight for the first couple of days until a kit's system gets used to the milk substitute and the shock of being parted from its mother. The amount fed will of course increase as the kit grows – and it will grow very fast – but never give so much milk that its stomach bloats. If a kit gets an upset stomach, take it right off milk and get a glucose-and-electrolyte solution from your vet, to be given for two or three feeds; then dilute it to 50:50 with milk substitute for a while, and gradually return to all milk substitute.

How?

You might have to teach the kit for the first feed or two. Wrap its body in a towel, with its head protruding (you will find it easier to hold that way, and the towel will stop its heavy head lolling about too much). Do not have the kit on its back; hold it at the sort of angle it would naturally assume if suckling from a jill. Handle it gently and talk softly; be in a quiet place with subdued lighting and no disturbance. With a drop of milk on it, coax the tip of the teat very gently into the kit's mouth, slightly off centre. Be prepared to take plenty of time over the first feed. The bottle rests comfortably in your hand and keeps warm. Do not force the kit if it really does not take to the teat: the more you struggle, the worse you will make it. As a last resort ask your vet for a 1 cc syringe with a blunt tip and insert it in the most comfortable position for the kit; dribble the liquid in very, very gradually and be extremely careful not to choke it. Remember that the kit is blind, deaf, helpless and motherless, and it is bound to be upset by alien smells, alien textures and alien noises.

Every time you feed, or shortly afterwards, you must stimulate the kit's bowels and bladder because its muscles are not yet developed. Stroke the stomach and back legs. Use cotton wool moistened in warm water to wipe its back end very gently until something happens – and it will probably urinate and defecate almost simultaneously. It may not defecate after every feed, but you must make sure that it passes water each time.

The mother would also lick the kit clean and you should use fresh moistened cotton wool to mop up its backside when it has defecated. Gently wash its tummy too, and wipe all traces of feed off its face before the milk supplement dries and causes bald patches. Pat the kit dry before you return it to the nestbox.

However carefully you attend to the bowel stimulation routine, some-one's likely to mess the box in the early days. Later on, when they start trying a little solid food, they will be careful to use one corner of the box for a latrine, but even then they will not have enough space to avoid the mess all the time. In the wild, of course, the jill is quick to keep her nest immaculately clean and the kits only defecate outside the nest once they have started on solid food.

How often?

For the first week, feed every two hours – *every* two hours, including nights. Then gradually reduce the number of night-time feeds over the next couple of weeks and at the same time begin to dilute the mixture slightly. (All changes should be made very gradually, whether in timing, amount of feed, strength of mixture, or introduction of new foods.) By three weeks old the feeds should be adjusted to every three or four hours and you can start offering a little solid food like finely minced tripe or raw meat scraped to a puree – just a very small amount twice a day. Be careful to remove any food which is not eaten.

By four weeks old their eyes might be beginning to open and they will become much more active over the next week or two and will need more space. Gradually increase the raw meat (you can start giving it whole rather than minced so they have something to chew at); reduce and dilute the bottle feeds and eventually replace them with milk supplement in a *shallow* dish (you don't want to drown them, and they will climb right in). Give them supervised access to fresh drinking-water as well, although they will probably not be interested while milk is available. Keep the dishes very clean and change the contents frequently. They have been used to sucking and it might take them a little while to learn how to lap: a little milk on the chin could encourage them. Add a little bonemeal to the meat to build up their bones and teeth. You could begin to add a very little wholemeal bread or puppymeal to the milk.

By five weeks old they should be capable of eating and drinking without assistance and they will be playing with each other. Give them an occasional day-old chick to eat, or perhaps a small mouse once their jaws are strong enough. Chewing on whole carcases will strengthen their jaws anyway.

They will need a bigger cardboard box now for exercising in, with sides high enough to prevent them from clambering out. Use some sawdust as litter on top of thick newspaper. Put them back into their nestbox for sleeping after a meal or when they are tired, and you probably will need a lid for safety's sake!

At six weeks old you can start to cut the milk right down as long as they are eating properly and drinking water. Their mother would begin to dry off her milk once they are more interested in meat and by eight weeks the milk can be stopped suddenly. They are ready to leave the pampering of the nursery and can move into proper hutches or join the commune. In a group situation make sure that they are not bullied at feeding time; they will soon learn to grab their fair share but may be a little timid at first.

Success

Mike Jasper, who set up the Surrey Ferret Society, succeeded in hand-rearing three kits from a litter of nine whose mother died within hours of their birth. He was lucky enough to have an understanding wife – anyone else might have divorced a man who got up every two hours during the night to bottlefeed ferrets! But those kits ended up as the most handled, tame and loyal ferrets he could every hope to have. Mike had to find his way by trial and error – hours-old orphans cannot wait for research – and his diary of the time makes interesting reading. It also makes you realize just what you might be letting yourself in for if you decide to hand-rear orphans!

Mike Jasper's Diary

28 May	9 kits born between 5 pm and 8.30 pm: 7m, 2f. Jill very weak.
	1 am: jill died.
	2 am: gave kits their first feed: 4 parts Shelley's Lactol powder to 10 parts water. Fed every two hours from then on.
29 May	7 pm: 2 males dead – never really took to bottle.
30 May	6 am: 3 more males dead, and all kits suffering from diarrhoea. Tried everything to stop the diarrhoea.
3 June	6.30 pm: 1 more male dead (diarrhoea). Left with 1 male, 2 females.
20 June	Still on 2-hourly feeds. Started giving finely minced tripe/meat.
22 June	Cut milk feed to every 3 hours.

27 June	Eyes starting to open. Cut feed to every 4 hours. (At last a good night's sleep!)
2 July	All three have their eyes open. Stopped bottlefeeding because they chew the teats off. All now eating meat/tripe/day-old chicks plus dish of Lactol.
23 July	Weaned by suddenly stopping milk.
30 July	Now running with hobs and jills in the commune.

(*Note:* The first four days were the worst – I found it difficult to keep to the feeding schedule, and the deaths did not help.)

SERIOUS BREEDING

Successful ferret breeding needs a good rapport with your jills, plenty of space for the growing young, the willingness to give them plenty of your time, the best of food for good growth and a basic understanding of genetics if you want to breed to particular conformations or colours.

Success! Mike Jasper with two of the orphans he successfully hand reared from birth.

Genetics is a complex subject but it boils down to the fact that each parent, through its genes, contributes certain characteristics to the offspring and it is the combinations of those characteristics that create the unique animal.

Some of these characteristics are said to be dominant, and some recessive, in relation to each other. Genes are paired in a fertilized egg – one from the father, one from the mother, for each characteristic – and the dominance or recessiveness of the genes determines the characteristics of the offspring that develops from the egg.

Take coat colour as an example. Let's describe a 'brown' coat as due to a dominant gene, C, and a 'white' coat as due to a recessive gene, c. If each parent supplies one C gene the offspring has the combination CC and its coat will be brown. If each parent supplies a different gene – one C and one c – the result (Cc or cC) is still brown, because of the presence of at least one dominant C gene in the pair. But if both parents supply one c gene each, the result (cc) is a *white* coat. Taking such a simple example, you will see that there are four possible gene pairs and that three of them result in the dominant colour, brown:

Father	Mother	Offspring	Colour
C	C	CC	Brown
C	c	Cc	Brown
c	C	cC	Brown
c	c	cc	White

This does *not* mean that if you cross two brown animals you necessarily get an all-brown litter. Each parent has *two* genes for each characteristic and one of them might have the recessive (c) gene in its genetic makeup (say cC or Cc, as in the second and third examples in the table above). That recessive gene will remain 'hidden' until it meets up with another recessive gene from a parent of the opposite sex, in which case an offspring (cc) will be the recessive colour, white. So if you breed from the brown animals Cc and cC in the table, there is a possibility of producing white offspring whose grandparents were brown.

The characteristic for albinism is carried by a *recessive* gene (and to complicate matters there may be more than one albino-type gene). So if you mate two pure pink-eyed albinos, you get nothing but albino kits. But if you mate any other colour with an albino, you might get a few albinos, or you might get no albinos at all if the mate does not happen to have a hidden recessive albino gene lurking on one of its chromosomes.

At present not enough work has been done systematically by breeders to establish ways of always breeding true to any colour other than albino and there is scope for some careful research by ferret clubs and specialists.

Breeding is also for conformation and character, and these are independent of colour, although some say that albinos are far more docile, and true first-cross hybrids between full-blooded wild polecats and any colour ferret are likely to be a great deal more agile and less manageable than an albino.

If you have the time and patience to breed selectively, you will find it immensely rewarding and interesting. Most people will simply put their favourite hob to their favourite jill and see what happens. The important thing is to avoid breeding from a genuinely bad animal, whether in temper, conformation or inherited health, because you will only perpetuate the undesirable trait. Ferret keepers are a long way from setting up the kind of breed registering societies that exist for commercial and rare farm livestock, but many already specialize in producing, say, 'greyhound' conformation types, fancy colours, very small jills, or whatever, and far too many people claim 'good working stock' – an advertising tag you should treat with suspicion! A good worker needs not just good breeding but also a good upbringing and good handling – and that is what keeping ferrets is all about.

8 Working Ferrets

RABBITS

Rabbits and ferrets seem to be a natural combination. It is likely that domesticated ferrets were introduced into Britain about the same time as rabbits, and specifically to help us with the hunting of them and to control them as pests on farmland. Rabbits were brought into this country to supply meat and fur and at first they were reared carefully in large warrens enclosed with banks topped by palisades or thorny shrubs. Artificial burrows and supplementary food were provided within the warren. Some of the inmates escaped and set up feral populations, which flourished, and eventually they became as much a nuisance as an asset. In 1340, for example, West Sussex wheatfields were recorded as being extensively damaged by rabbits. In theory a single doe, producing five litters a year with five young in each, could be responsible for generating more than 4,500 rabbits in three years. Population increases were greatly assisted later by the policy of protecting game birds by waging war on natural predators like foxes, stoats, weasels and polecats.

Thirty or forty years ago the wild rabbit population in Britain was substantial and people could earn a living from the animals. In 1948, for example, the annual catch in England and Wales was estimated at 60–100 *million* wild rabbits. Ferrets were kept in every countryman's shed and quite a few town backyards, and a day's ferreting was a regular way of supplementing the family's diet and income.

Then in the early 1950s myxomatosis arrived with a vengeance. It was first seen in Britain in the summer of 1953 and by the end of 1954 it was countrywide. Ninety-nine per cent of the rabbit population was wiped out. Others have written about that horrifying epidemic and those who witnessed the sight of fields and fields of stricken rabbits will never forget that first ferocious year.

In Britain the disease was carried by the rabbit flea, which breeds in burrows where the does give birth and suckle their young. Normally underground warrens are large and crowded, and 'myxy' could spread very fast indeed right through the population. In 1953 a small percentage of British rabbits was for some reason living above ground, in solitary nests, hare-like. They were outcasts and would usually be less than successful rabbits, more vulnerable to predators. This open living, however, protected them from the ravages of myxy and enough of them survived to contribute eventually to a rally in the rabbit population. Gradually the

British strain of the myxy virus mutated (no virus can survive if *all* its host are killed), mortality decreased and those that survived gained a certain degree of immunity. In south and central America, the original source of the virus, where it occurs naturally in some of the native wild rabbit species, affected animals merely suffer a temporary lump on the infected site, and it may be that eventually this will be the case in Britain. But the American rabbits and their virus have lived together long enough to develop a balance between them.

The disappearance of rabbits from England's chalk downlands had dramatic effects on the character of the vegetation. The familiar sweep of lawnlike turf with occasional bushes became an unkempt wilderness with dense swards of grass and tangles of brambles. It also affected the wildlife: hares increased in numbers, and foxes switched to hunting voles, mice, poultry and game birds. Partridges became more scarce: the lack of rabbits led to a lack of short herbage where ants could thrive, and ants are a major source of food for partridge chicks.

It takes a lot to wipe out rabbits! Australia suffered enormously from plagues of them. They were originally introduced in 1859 for sport and soon there was an export trade worth several million pounds a year in meat to Britain and fur to the United States. But with no natural predators the rabbits quickly became out-of-control pests, devastating grazing lands. Myxy was introduced from South America as a form of biological control; it failed in its task in 1936 but succeeded dramatically in 1950. The Australian virus was carried by mosquitoes, not fleas, and initial mortality among rabbits was 99.5 per cent. One million square miles were affected during the first summer, and sheep-wool production alone was increased by £34 million.

In the 1980s British farmers are once again concerned about damage by rabbits and some consider that numbers are high enough to be a considerable threat to crops in some parts of the country. In 1984 the destruction of British crops was estimated to cost tens of millions and it is feared that the animals' increasing resistance to myxy (50 per cent of stricken rabbits can now survive the disease) could have grave and costly consequences. Some farmers, especially those who are more concerned with agribusiness than agriculture, are launching all-out war against the resilient lagomorph, and their arsenal includes some formidable weapons.

It is ironic that, in a society which recognizes the health benefits of low-fat diets, potentially valuable wild rabbit meat is wantonly wasted. Rabbit meat offers a higher percentage of protein, less fat and less moisture than poultry, veal, beef, lamb or pork. It also contains less calories per pound. It is a very good food. Why is it wasted?

In the past rabbit warrens were an *asset*, and full-time warreners were employed to ensure a continuing supply of rabbit meat for the table and the market. There are gamekeepers alive today who started their careers as warreners. Old Vic, for example, recalled catching 31,000 rabbits in his first year as a full-time warrener; the butcher's lorry called two or three times a week for the estate's surplus. The rabbits were caught in gin-traps (now illegal); culling was by rotation, an area would be selected, gins set at the entrance of every hole – perhaps three or four hundred of them – and Old Vic would go out at 11 pm to pick up whatever he had caught in the gins. As he emptied each trap he would reset it – and would hear it catching a fresh victim as he moved down the line. In those pre-myxy days he could take six or seven hundred rabbits in a night and at sixpence a rabbit he could make seven or eight pounds on top of his basic wage of ten and sixpence a week. The rabbit population was controlled and exploited and the estate had an excellent source of income. Gradually the warrens were cleared out and finally the estate stopped employing warreners. Almost immediately, the rabbit population exploded. Then came the myxy.

Today landowners gas the warrens and untold mountains of good cheap rabbit meat are poisoned and wasted. There is ample potential for farming the rabbits rather than destroying them. Unproductive areas of land would be ideal for enclosed warrens and the returns could be substantial if marketing techniques were developed. Rabbit meat is much too good to waste.

If a landowner does prefer to exterminate than harvest his rabbits, he has ready access to the means of mass slaughter. Gassing is highly lethal and very efficient, but it kills *everything* that happens to be underground at the time (including foxes, badgers, stoats and domestic cats) and it leaves all that inedible meat rotting down below. The substances used in gassing are dangerous to handle and there is no way of knowing just how unpleasant a death is experienced by the unseen victims. Lamping, or night shooting, is another efficient method of slaughter, and it has the advantage of being more selective. Snaring is far too time-consuming to be an effective way of controlling large numbers of rabbits these days, but a snared rabbit is a clean one, free from poison and free from shot. However, snaring is indiscriminate: snares take whatever happens to enter them.

Ferreting is nothing to do with extermination. Ferreting to nets is just about the only form of rabbiting that is completely selective and gives you good, clean rabbits for your own pot or for your local butcher or game dealer. You have the choice of killing or releasing what you catch in the net; you do not waste meat, and you also get a day's sport and some exercise for your ferret. And that is why people go ferreting.

> The hunter knows the world he lives in as few others do and he lives in sympathy with it rather than trying to dominate it. He is the best of conservationists, knowing exactly how much he can take from where at any given time. To overhunt is considered one of the major crimes, in the nature of a sin . . .

This quotation comes from *The Mountain People*, Colin Turnbull's account of the way of life of the Ik people in Uganda. The Ik were hunter-gatherers, until bureaucracy decided otherwise and forced them to settle, and they lived in harmony with the environment, respecting the wildlife, harvesting it carefully, taking only what they needed to eat, never killing for the sake of doing so, understanding thoroughly the ways of wild animals. That is the art of the good hunter, whether you are an Ik ranging far and wide in the Ugandan mountains or a ferreter seeking a day's sport along a railway embankment.

R.M. Lockley's *The Private Life of the Rabbit* and John Marchington's *Pugs and Drummers* tell the rabbit hunter most of what he needs to know about his prey. Both books are well worth studying. Ferreting is never straightforward (that is one of its attractions) and it helps to know as much as you can about rabbits, who rarely do what you expect or hope they will do. The experiences of other people might give you a few ideas and hints, but no book or advice can take the place of personal experience – your own 'feel'.

This book offers basic guidelines for those new to the sport but does not presume to teach you all about ferreting – we do not want to spoil your fun in finding out from experience! Our plea is that you should not waste what you kill and should only kill what you need. If you have no use for its meat, release the rabbit from your net and let it go free. You still have your sport and you still have a good excuse to be out in the countryside on a winter's morning.

Preparations

Ferreting needs forethought and you should start planning long before you acquire your ferrets. Unless you are a poacher (and very few people are so hungry these days that they actually need to poach) your first priority is to be granted access to rabbits. And it is not going to be easy. More and more people seek to enjoy a few hours of casual country sports, and there are less and less opportunities for practising them. Landowners and game-keepers are inundated with requests from people wanting access to their land for ferreting, rough shooting or whatever.

Remember that you are seeking a *favour* and it is up to you to prove that you are worthy of it. Far too many people abuse the privilege, take more than they have been granted, make a nuisance of themselves by leaving gates open, damaging fencing, upsetting pheasants and livestock, leaving snares, letting their dogs run amok, littering the land with car-tridges, alarming the neighbours, losing their ferrets, proving generally untrustworthy and worse. Not surprisingly, farmers and keepers are wary of letting people on to their land! They have had bad experiences with the most plausible characters; they have had ample reasons to regret giving certain people as much as the time of day. Ferrets have for generations been associated with poaching and the image is a difficult one to live down, especially as many ferreters are secretly quite pleased with that image.

You will have to earn your privileges: there is no need to bootlick but do not be pushy or arrogant; take the trouble to prove to a keeper that you are genuine, keen, trustworthy and helpful. Offer him your time and will-ing labour and show that you are completely reliable and honest. Do not resent it if he checks out your background (and your family's) with the local police. Be prepared to be helpful for several months before you presume to ask about such favours as ferreting rights. Understand that some keepers (if they have spare time – which is unlikely) enjoy a spot of rabbiting themselves and might not want to share their hard-earned sport. A keeper's life is sheer hard work, long unsociable hours, a relentless day-in day-out series of routines that give no quarter to Sundays, filthy weather or hangovers. Such a man is going to demand as much of you as of himself.

If you can acquire your ferrets from a keeper in the first place, so much the better. You immediately have something in common and he will be aware that one day you are going to want some ferreting.

Farmers are as wary as keepers. If they have a rabbit problem on the farm there are much more efficient ways of dealing with it than letting any Tom, Dick or Harry and their ferrets run riot over the land. Ferreters are not doing the farmer any favours, unless they can establish a good working relationship in which they have a regular responsibility to control rabbits (rather than exterminate them) because the farmer has neither the time nor inclination to do so himself. It won't hurt your chances with a farmer if you help with humping straw bales when the pressure is on, or make yourself useful at haymaking.

Once you have been granted access, never abuse the privilege. However open the arrangement seems to be, always make sure the farmer or keeper knows when and where you are going ferreting, remind him you are there and let him know when you have finished for the day. Leave no trace of your activities. Pick up *all* your nets (livestock can suffer if you don't). Have a clear agreement about whether you may bring a dog or a gun and also what happens to the bag. You should not just assume that the kill is yours, and you should anyway have the courtesy to leave a brace at the back door for the house.

The site

Get to know your land intimately and spend plenty of time observing the rabbits before you do anything about them. When you are ready to tackle a particular site, it may be necessary to clear a bit of undergrowth a few days before you try ferreting. Rabbits often have bury entrances in among the brambles and that does not help net-setting. It is no good leaving the clearance until the day you go rabbiting. Ferreting is essentially a silent operation; the rabbits pick up any unusual sounds and then they won't budge from the safety of the bury.

Check that the site is actively inhabited. There is characteristic vegetation associated with rabbitries, consisting of plants which the rabbits find distasteful and which flourish where the soil levels of phosphorus and nitrogen are high because of rabbit droppings and urine. Typical plants left untouched by rabbits, where everything else is often cropped very short or the ground is bare, are elder, ragwort (poisonous to cattle), stinging nettle and mullein, all of which tend to be found growing in warrens.

Rabbits also leave plants like clustered bellflower, rockrose, salad burnet, sandwort, wild forget-me-not, thistle and the very poisonous henbane. Plants which are palatable but which can withstand rabbit grazing include wild thyme, self-heal and eyebright. A typical area grazed heavily by rabbits has tight springy turf and a fair bit of bare earth and ragwort.

Signs of present habitation include *fresh* droppings and a definite smell of rabbit, but even the most obvious signs can turn out to be misleading and the rabbits are tucked away down holes that look as if no one has been near them for months. If you have a good dog, he will soon let you know where the rabbits are at home.

Encounters

Rabbit holes give refuge to more than rabbits and your ferret could come across foxes, badgers, snakes, weasels, stoats, rats, cats and even little owls. Most of them get out quick if a ferret is about. Weasels and stoats prefer avoidance to confrontation, although some people say that feral ferrets will mate with their cousinly stoats. Foxes and cats usually leave rapidly, and with some irritation, but a badger is quite capable of lashing out at an impudent ferret and killing it. Ferrets, like terriers, are no respecters of size, power and temper.

There is a nice film sequence of a fox having a lazy scratch on a warm day on a streamside track in Cambridgeshire. An old badger ambles along, intent on distant business. In passing, and apparently without breaking his stride, he fetches the fox a wallop that lands it in the ditch before it even knows the badger is around. Close-up of startled, bedraggled fox, crestfallen about the ears, clambering out of the ditch and getting the hell out of there. No one gets in the way of a grumpy badger.

Equipment

Ferreting easily becomes an expedition. In theory you should be able to pop a couple of ferrets in one pocket and a few nets in the other, clamber over the field gate and start working. In practice you will probably find yourself carrying a lot more gear than that.

Ferreting to nets is quiet and efficient. It can be done by one man on his own with no help from anyone except his ferrets. The rabbits he catches will be killed cleanly with a quick neckbreak and he has the choice of exercising mercy by releasing those that are too young, in milk, or otherwise unwanted. He will use purse nets.

A *purse net* has a drawstring running around its circumference and through rings at opposite ends of the net. It is designed to be spread over a rabbit hole, with the drawstring pegged to the ground at one end. When

Carrying box, 'dollybag', nets, bleeper, graft, ferret – and hip flask!

a rabbit bolts out from the hole, its impetus immediately draws the net into a bag or purse around it. The peg sometimes holds the bundle more or less in place until you get to the victim to dispatch or release it, but you must act fast.

You can make your own nets or you can buy them from any sporting shop or agricultural merchants. Readymade nets are either nylon or hemp and usually come in two sizes: 3½ or 4 ft (1 m or 1.2 m). Talk to your supplier – most people use the 3½-ft (1 m) size. They come in a variety of colours, depending on the background against which the rabbit will see them – or, rather, not see them. The mesh is just big enough for a ferret to pass through, unless it stops for a scratch and gets in a tangle. Hemp will last for many years if you take proper care of it and some people find it easier to handle than nylon, although nylon is lighter, virtually indestructible and needs less careful drying and storing.

Every time that you use a net, check that its drawstring is running freely before you set out. Slip a finger into each ring and stretch the net lengthwise between your hands to see if it snarls. To pick up at the end of a session, clear out any debris from the mesh, hook a finger through each ring and pull them apart so that the net is drawn tidily into a length. Fold it neatly two or three times and wrap the drawstring around the bundle. As soon as you come home, hang the nets out in an airy place to dry completely before you store them away. Nets are valuable: treat them properly and they will last.

Folding a net. Hook your fingers into the two rings and draw them apart so that the mesh lies tidily and is not tangled. Fold the net, end to end, a couple of times and then wind the drawstring around the bundle to secure it.

Always count your nets out and count them in again at the end of a session; they are easily overlooked as they lie in place. Some people have a rubber band round each net and slip the band on to the wrist as the net is set out. If you are still wearing rubber bands on the way home, you have left some nets behind. Banded nets are handy spares when the action gets going: they can be released very quickly and set over a gaping hole in no time.

You can never have enough purse nets. The initial outlay is expensive but you need to be ready to cover every single escape hole on the site – the rabbits are bound to use the one you failed to net. A dozen nets might just be enough for the smallest bury but twenty is better, and if you are ferreting regularly you will probably build up a stock of two or three score.

Pegs are needed for securing purse nets. They usually come with the nets. They can be bought separately for very little, but most people make their own from hazel. If you have dipped the top ends in a pot of light-coloured paint, it makes finding the nets at the end of the session that much easier.

Long nets are a different art. They are used as backstops, set up several yards away from the bury to foil bolting rabbits so that guns or dogs have a chance of taking them. Long nets are usually a yard wide and can be anything from twelve to a hundred yards long. They can be awkward to handle, especially in a strong wind, and they are often used at night.

A *graft spade* is considered essential by many people. It is used for digging out rabbits when your ferret has killed down in the bury and refuses to come out, which is something that can happen with the best and most reliable ferret on occasion. Some people do not believe in digging and are content to wait or come back later for the ferret, but most will not want to leave a good rabbit down the hole. The graft blade is long, narrow and curved and a good size is about 6 ins (15 cm) across the top of the blade, tapering to about 5 ins (12.5 cm) at the bottom and curving an inch out of true. The blade is about 12 ins (30 cm) long and the handle a couple of feet. It is also a useful tool for blocking bury entrances if you are gassing. You can buy collapsible grafts for easier carrying but they are expensive and the blades are small enough to make digging very tedious.

You can take a length of *steel rod* with you as a sounding device unless you are using bleepers. If the ferret is 'laid up', push one end of the rod into the ground and put your ear against the other end. You will hear a rabbit's scratchings. Keep resiting the rod and with a little skill you will be able to pinpoint its position exactly for digging. Experts don't need such aids: they put an ear to the hole and can judge exactly where the digging should start.

A *ferret finder* or *bleeper* is the high-tech way of locating a lost or wilful ferret. It is an electronic device: a small transmitter is fitted on a collar around the ferret's neck and you have a receiver in your hand which bleeps like a metal detector or a geiger-counter. The device is expensive but it is accurate and can save hours of misdirected digging and frustration.

A *line* is a ten- or twelve-yard length of non-twist cord. It is attached to the collar of a *liner*, which is a big, strong, bossy, antisocial hob ferret whose job is to go by the shortest route to a ferret that has killed down in the bury and is laid up with the kill. The liner, who lives a solitary life, drives the ferret off the kill and then stays put. You can thus locate the kill by following his line, and dig down to retrieve the rabbit and the liner. If you mark the cord at intervals in some way, you will know how far down the liner is. Put a special mark a yard from the liner's end so that you know when he is within arm's reach. Some people knot the cord but you do not want it to snag on obstructions. Alternatively, a liner could be fitted with a bleeper.

The *carrier* in which you will transport your ferrets is an important piece of equipment and should be chosen with care. For the sake of the

A good carrying box: two separate compartments, each with a sliding lid.

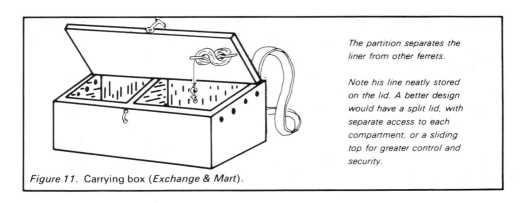

The partition separates the liner from other ferrets.

Note his line neatly stored on the lid. A better design would have a split lid, with separate access to each compartment, or a sliding top for greater control and security.

Figure 11. Carrying box (*Exchange & Mart*).

ferrets it should be comfortable, weatherproof, well-ventilated, well-insulated, familiar and visible in the field. For your sake it should be easy to carry over long distances and rough terrain. For the sake of the ferreting it should muffle the excited scrabblings of ferrets eager to get on with the job. For the sake of general convenience it should be designed so that you can take out the ferret or ferrets of your choice without the whole lot escaping.

The usual carriers are boxes, bags or sacks. Forget the sacks; they are easy to carry and they muffle the scrabbling but they get wet if left in the rain or on the ground, they give no protection in cold weather, they are suffocating in hot weather, they are difficult to keep clean, they are easily worried into an escape hole by the ferret, and, very seriously, they are too easily trodden on in the heat of the moment.

A really stout canvas dollybag is a possibility. Give it a solid base so that it can be stood on the ground without absorbing moisture or falling over and put in some hay or straw for comfort. Make sure it has good ventilation holes but check that they have secure metal eyelets and cannot be worked at by a ferret eager to come out before it should. A good tough dollybag can be carried quite conveniently and it can be hung on a branch to keep it off the ground and out of harm's way and, incidentally, in the shade. Its main drawback is in removing the ferret of your choice. Nor is it easy to devise a compartment system for a liner.

All sorts of boxes have been devised. They can be bought or you can make your own to suit your needs. They have a lot of advantages. From the point of view of the ferret, boxes are secure, comfortable and much like home. Unlike a bag or sack, a box can be left by the bury overnight if you lose your ferret, and in the morning he'll be curled up inside it sound asleep. The box must be big enough for the number of ferrets you take, remembering that during a day's ferreting each animal will need rest periods between working bouts. 2 ft 6 ins × 1 ft × 9 ins (75 cm × 30 cm × 23 cm) would be big enough for two ferrets and a liner, with an internal compartment to isolate the liner.

Plywood makes it light enough to be carried but make sure the structure is strong. Most people prefer to design and make their own carriers (that's half the challenge of keeping ferrets) but there are fibreglass boxes on the market which claim to be light and strong and to muffle scrabbling effectively. Wooden boxes can be a little noisy and need to be left well away from the buries.

Drill some ventilation holes not more than 1 in. (2.5 cm) across near the top of the box. The roof should be a securely fastened split lid, so that you can open either compartment and reach in for the selected ferret. A sliding roof gives you better control than a hinged lid. Add fresh bedding every time you go ferreting. Make a comfortably broad carrying strap; narrow ones soon cut into your shoulders. If you are a fancy carpenter you could shape the back of the box so that it fits you more snugly as you walk, or it might be worth fixing a pad to it. By the time you are encumbered with spades, bleepers, hip flasks and rabbits, you will appreciate a light and comfortable ferret carrier for the homeward trudge.

Ferret carriers should always be placed out of direct sunlight. Even in winter the container could become warm enough for heatstroke. Check the position frequently – the sun has a strange habit of moving!

Refreshment is another necessity. Apart from your own, you must carry some milk or water for the ferrets and perhaps a suitable small drinking dish (or your cupped hand will do). Ferreting is thirsty work and a thirsty ferret might travel considerable distances underground in search of water.

A sharp *knife* is a vital part of your equipment of course, especially for paunching and legging the rabbits. You need one with a good point to it. Take a tool for cutting undergrowth if you can carry it.

Gloves are useful for undergrowth but not for ferrets. You have trained your ferret to know your hand, not your glove, and you should feel confident enough to be able to stick your hand down a hole to find out what is going on without any fear that your ferret could mistake your hand for something else in the heat of the moment.

Dogs are a useful part of the team if they know the ferrets and know their job. You need a quiet, good-natured and wholly reliable dog, guaranteed not to bark or get restless. If a puppy and a ferret have been raised together, they will work well together. Steadiness is essential: in the excitement of the bolt you do not want the dog mistaking your best ferret for an escaping rabbit. You cannot *train* a dog to be of use for ferreting but a good animal will sense what you require of it, which is primarily to

ABOVE: A good, steady dog is useful for marking occupied buries, and for retrieving the ones that nearly got away.   BELOW: Dog and ferret should be brought up together and should know each other well.

mark holes that are occupied by rabbits so that you know where to enter your ferrets. If no guns are being used, a dog comes in handy for the occasional rabbit that comes from the hidden pophole you failed to net.

Bells, bootlaces, muzzles and other bits are unnecessary. You can still buy ferret bells, the theory being that a belled ferret can be more easily located down under, but they hardly help the ferret. Bootlaces have been recommended by some for attaching to a ferret's collar, one end trailing loose, so that if the animal does not readily come to hand you have a chance of putting a quick foot on the end of the lace and holding him there. You would do far better to have a ferret that has been handled properly and will not mess you about.

Muzzles we would sum up in a word: don't! The old books go into elaborate details about muzzles - leather ones, rod-and-ring ones, whip-cord copes and so on. The intention, of course, is to deter the ferret from killing down. But pause to consider what would happen to a muzzled ferret if it met something other than a rabbit in the bury, or if it was lost. It can't fend for itself.

Nor is a muzzled ferret any less likely to lie up than an unmuzzled ferret. If it has a rabbit up a dead end it will scrabble away with its claws because it cannot use its teeth, whereas unmuzzled it might kill quickly and move off to get on with its work, particularly if it is a properly fed ferret.

The essence of ferreting should be simplicity and the less you encumber yourself and the ferret the better for both of you. Let it work as naturally as possible. If you respect your ferret, handle it well, feed it sensibly, refrain from overworking it to the point of tiredness or boredom - in short, if you *know* your ferret and are on its wavelength - lie-ups and digging-out will be rare events and ferreting will be a much more satisfying business altogether. The only essential equipment is your nets, your ferrets and your ears.

The ferrets

Everyone has their own ideas about the best ferrets for rabbiting, and the best combinations. It is as personal as an angler choosing the right flies. Take at least two ferrets, so that each has a chance to rest now and again. In a large bury you will need two loose ferrets working simultaneously as a team underground, and possibly more according to circumstances. Try with a pair at first and add more if necessary.

The aim of ferreting is that the ferret should force the rabbit to bolt out of the safety of its bury. Rabbits have an instinctive fear of mustelids, and mustelids have an instinct for going down any and every hole. Ferrets hunt for the sake of hunting and it makes no difference at all if they are well fed: they still have the urge to explore and hunt, and the rabbit is not going to stop and ask whether the ferret has any intention of eating it. The ideal working ferret enjoys ferreting about and loses interest in a rabbit once it is dead. Many dogs are the same: it is the pursuit that they relish and a dead rabbit does not run.

It is absolutely unnecessary to starve a ferret before working. A starved ferret is much more likely to kill down and lie up – that is, to kill a rabbit in the bury and then stay with it for a meal followed by a long snooze, in which case you risk losing the rabbit, the ferret, the daylight and your temper. Feed according to the normal timetable, but allow an hour for digestion before setting the ferret to work, and give it a snack during the day to keep up its stamina and as a reward for all its hard work.

Whatever your choice, you want a *willing* ferret that enjoys its work, and you should be alert to any flagging of energy or interest. Some people only use jills; some prefer a hob. Some like a very lively worker; others prefer a quieter animal in the belief that it is less likely to *catch* a rabbit, and it is possible that the albino was favoured by the old breeders for just this quality of docility. An advantage of an albino is that a white coat is easily seen, so that there is less chance of the ferret wandering off along the hedgerow unnoticed. Ferrets are great wanderers, following their noses and their fancies to nowhere in particular. In practice all your senses are at such a high pitch of expectation when you are ferreting that you will immediately be aware of the slightest movement above ground, whatever the colour of your ferret.

If you are using bleepers on loose working ferrets, you may not need a liner hob to locate a lie-up, although he will still come in useful for chasing off the sitting ferret. There are drawbacks to bleepers and to liners. The bleeper collar could snag on an underground obstruction; and batteries have been known to fail. We have also heard of a receiver acting very positively all over the bury which, as it turned out, was not because of an exceptionally active ferret but because the operator forgot that he had a spare transmitter in his own pocket! The capital outlay on a bleeper could be ten times the price of a young liner hob, but you do not have to feed and house a bleeper and it does pinpoint the ferret's position precisely. A liner can take a twisting course (because the bury does) so that it is laborious to locate him; he can get his line entangled on snags; he can make a meal of the kill before you can dig down to rescue it; he can be difficult to handle; and he must always be housed separately from other ferrets. If you do need a bossy hob to chase out loose ferrets, you can put a bleeper on him rather than a line.

The biggest drawback of a bleeper could be the very fact that it is so accurate. It pinpoints the ferret nicely. As you thrust your spade once again into the solid ground, it suddenly finds the tunnel and, meeting no resistance from the soil, it plunges in sharply – straight on top of the ferret. If, on the other hand, you are using a line it may be more long-winded but at least you know where the tunnel is; and if you have marked the line as suggested you know when your ferret is within arm's length, so that you can dig to the mark without the risk of chopping into its skull.

Novice ferrets

A young novice ferret needs a little help. You will of course have been handling it from an early age, preferably as soon as it starts coming out of the nest and before its eyes are open, and that is the major part of any training it needs for ferreting. It must be completely familiar with your hands so that you can pick it up easily whatever the situation and with luck can teach it to come to your call or whistle.

During the handling, encourage a youngster to explore pipes, disused or artificial buries, wellington boots and so on. It will not need much encouraging – any opening is usually irresistible, including an open-ended shirtsleeve. But you should also teach it to come to hand. When the real work begins you want a ferret that has no objection to being plucked out of a hole; it should not back off and disappear underground again, nor should it attack your reaching hand! If you do some preliminary work in pipes or empty buries, let the ferret have some uninterrupted explorations but also practise pulling it out and putting it in again. Take plenty of time. If you can encourage it to come to your call or whistle, so much the better. A soft clucking or chirrup is useful – it is less likely to disturb rabbits. Another useful sound, particularly at feeding time, is a gently rattled stick; when you are ferreting, a stick rattled at the entrance of the hole should bring out the ferret, for the sake of curiosity, when you want him.

The next stage is to introduce the youngster to the real world. Choose a small bury where you know there is a rabbit or two at home. Take an experienced jill – preferably the youngster's mother – and let her show the novice what to do. He may be a little timid at first but his curiosity will soon get the better of him when the jill disappears underground. Give him time. He is there to learn. Let him explore thoroughly. If he emerges from a hole, put him back in the hole where you *originally* entered him. Your aim is to encourage him to come right out of a hole when he has finished, rather than peeking a nose out and disappearing down again, and if you simply push him back into the hole he is emerging from he will soon decide to push himself back instead and stay down there. The last thing you want is a shy ferret which will not come to hand, and such behaviour could result in habitual lying-up. If a novice does lie up, dig immediately so that it will learn not to do so.

You should use purse nets, not guns, for novice sessions. Although on its first encounter it may well be shy of pushing through a net, a youngster needs to learn that it can slip quite easily through the mesh. Use a practice net at home so that it becomes a familiar object in a familiar environment before you introduce the youngster to a whole new world.

When to work

The ferreting season is traditionally in the winter months, for several reasons. There is less undergrowth to impede you in winter, and there is less risk of heatstroke for the ferrets or flies on the rabbit meat. There should also be less likelihood of a bury full of very young rabbits, which make too easy a catch for the ferret and are not the sort of rabbit for your bag anyway. However, rabbits now seem to breed all year round, although winter is a quieter time. The old rule was only to go ferreting when there was an R in the month, and most people prefer to start some time in October and finish by March.

There are many theories about the ideal weather conditions for ferreting. Most people like a quiet, frosty day, starting very early in the morning. A drawback of a deep frost is that footsteps can resonate on iron-hard ground and give due warning to the rabbits. A settled day after a snowfall which has started to freeze is likely to be more productive than a muggy, heavy afternoon; rabbits tend to sit tight in the bury in damp, muggy weather. Some say that no rabbit will bolt in snow or in wet and windy weather, but that could be just an excuse for staying indoors. There are plenty of theories about waxing and waning moons, equinoxes and so on. In the end you will develop a sixth sense about when to go ferreting. That is one of the privileges of experience, but even then the rabbits will laugh in your face and refuse to bolt for no apparent reason. And if they insist on staying down, so will your ferrets.

Myxy and ferreting do not mix. Although the disease is much milder these days, most populations have recurrent epidemics in quite regular cycles – perhaps every three years. Myxy rabbits tend to stay above ground, which is no good at all for ferreting. And if you start killing off the healthy ones among them, you are not giving the community a chance to build up again. Ferreting is nothing to do with extermination.

Where

Your options are of course limited according to the access you are granted.

Obviously it is more laborious to work in a bramble patch or an overgrown area of woodland. The easiest buries are shallow warrens in sand; digging out is light work but there is a risk of a cave-in suffocating your ferret. The typical chalk downland warrens provide plenty of challenge; the old ones often go very deep into the hillside and have 'shelves' (a second tunnel running above and parallel to the first) up to which the rabbit jumps for safety, leaving the ferret to continue merrily along the main run. Digging into chalk is sheer hard work, which is as good a reason as any for leaving your graft at home. On the other hand, downland warrens are often easy to net; the visibility is usually good, and the scenery pleasant. There is more to ferreting than sport.

Burrow systems can be very complicated, at several different levels with a maze (or warren!) of interconnected passages, a lot of escape routes and plenty of dead ends once used as nesting chambers. New nesting chambers are dug out by the does for each litter and tend to be deep into the warren for safety. It is these dead ends that cause the most lie-ups: the rabbit is trapped by the ferret and hunches its body, head against the end of the run. If the ferret cannot reach the rabbit's neck for a kill, it will scrabble with its claws and teeth at the rabbit's back end in an attempt to climb over it and go for the jugular. A small ferret might be able to climb over, spend less time about killing and cause less damage, pain and terror to the rabbit.

Lie-ups also occur in the passage when a fast ferret surprises a rabbit and kills before it has a chance to bolt. If the ferret is a good one, and if it is small, it will kill and then move on by climbing over the carcase.

If you suspect that the warren is well established (some are centuries old) and rambling, you must be prepared to use several ferrets. Even a pair will not have much chance of success: the rabbits know every twist of every tunnel and will lead the ferrets an endless and exhausting chase underground with never a need to leave the safety of the buries. A team of ferrets will be more successful in bolting them.

How

One of the pleasures of ferreting is that it is an art rather than a science. We are not presuming to tell you more than the basic principles. Then you can have the satisfaction of finding out the many secrets of the art for yourself. However, Fred J. Taylor's excellent book, *Shooting Times Guide to Ferreting*, will help you considerably.

The essence of ferreting is silence: footsteps rumble like thunder through a warren and the sound of human voices resounds in the corridors; bury entrances act like radio receiver bowls to catch the slightest under-the-breath swearing from several yards away and magnify it magnificently; and the very efficient design of the rabbit's large ears increases the magnification and range of sound capture. Tread very gently; use sign language if you have a partner; do not whimper if you are a dog; and avoid cracking twigs and leaves with your boots. Act with stealth, and take them by surprise. If the rabbits know you are there, not even the fear of a ferret will make them bolt. Remember that their sense of smell is as acute as their hearing; keep the right side of the wind and leave your cigarettes at home.

Net-setting

You must net every single hole, however small and unused it seems to be. One or two emergency popholes are usually a little way out from the main bury, often hidden under leaves and grass. They are almost vertical exits from flat ground, rather than the normal hole excavated into a slope. Use a prodstick to see if a hole is a hole or just an abandoned scrape leading nowhere.

Set the net carefully over the hole with one ring at the bottom and the other ring at the top. To start with you will find it easier to rest the bottom ring just inside the mouth of the hole, because this will help the net to form the beginnings of a slight purse shape. Spread the net so that it completely covers the hole, with no sneaky gaps at the sides for the rabbit's escape. Push the drawstring peg into the ground above the hole.

Net every hole and have spare nets in your pocket so that you can cover the hole immediately with a new net when a rabbit has been caught in the original and another one is close behind. It is common for more than one rabbit to bolt from the same hole in quick succession.

Be prepared to spend a lot of time setting up the nets; it is fiddly but worthwhile. You will not need nets if you are bolting to the gun but netting gives you clean rabbits for the table, and purse nets and ferrets have worked well together for centuries.

Patience

Start by working the lower holes of the slope. Let the dog mark the occupied holes for you. Lift the edge of a net, slip in a ferret, and replace the net carefully. Stand well back; take a downwind position above the hole so that a potential bolter can neither see nor smell you and change its mind about bolting. Then wait. And listen. If after a while your hear the rabbits moving below and your ferret does not show, they are probably leading him a merry dance and he needs help. Enter another ferret to help him sort them out.

Setting the nets: *1* Place the lower ring just inside the mouth of the hole.

2 Push the peg into the ground above the hole.

3 Spread out the edges of the purse net to cover the exit completely. The net should be slightly bagged.

4 Nets ready.

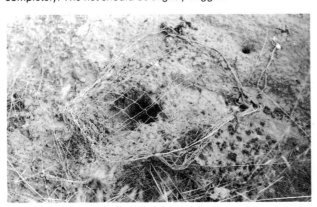

5 Popholes are usually small, insignificant and easily overlooked, but they must be netted. Many a rabbit owes its freedom to an un-netted pophole.

Entering a ferret.

Give your ferrets plenty of time to search the warren but have all your senses on full alert. When the action happens, it is sudden, fast and exciting, and you need to respond immediately.

Trust your ferrets. They may show a nose at another hole and disappear again; leave them alone. One might just pop out for a quick scratch against the rim of the hole, give a quick shake, and turn back in again. If one slips out and starts wandering, pick it up before it disrupts the net and pop it in again, replacing the net carefully. Try another hole if it persists in emerging after only a few moments. If your dog says there are rabbits down there, keep trying, but the ferret probably knows better than the dog. If all your ferrets show, respect their unanimous decision. Think ferret and move on a few holes. With a little experience you will be able to tell how much interconnection there is between holes, and whether there is more than one system of buries.

If you are working a hedgerow, ferret up the hedge and upwind. When a rabbit slips back into a hole behind you, do not bother to go back to that hole; he knows you are there and will not come out again.

Action

Suddenly you hear a thundering noise like a herd of underground buffalo. The earth vibrates under your feet and a rabbit bursts out of a hole, slamming into the net. Get there quick: put your foot over the gaping hole in case another one is on the way (don't tread on your ferret!), disentangle the rabbit if there is time, despatch it quickly and cleanly, re-set the net and wait for another. The force of the rabbit's exit will have drawn the net into a bag around him, and quite often he will have pulled out the peg so that the bundle begins to tumble away. Alternatively his reactions are so fast that he immediately attempts to get back down the hole, net and all, and you must grab him quickly. Also the natural inclination of any sensible pursuing ferret, given half a chance, is to drag the prey back down into the hole. Food is meant to be stored – and eaten – underground.

If the rabbits are really on the move, keep a foot on the bagged rabbit's neck and set a spare net over the hole before you deal with him.

Despatch

Hold the rabbit by the back legs while you disentangle it from the net. Take care – it will struggle for its life.

The quickest, surest and most humane methods of killing a rabbit are the neck-pull and the chin-up. With your palm turned towards the rabbit's head, take its neck either between finger and thumb or between your first and second fingers. Stretch the neck by pulling the head slightly upwards

LEFT: Bagged rabbit.
BELOW: Disentangling the
rabbit. OPPOSITE PAGE: Humane
despatch – the neck-pull
method. (*above*) Take the
rabbit's neck between your
index and middle fingers.
(*below*) Push the chin sharply
up and back as you stretch the
neck to break it quickly.

and backwards, taking the strain by retaining a firm grip with your other
hand on the hind legs, until you feel and hear the unmistakable dislocation
of the rabbit's neck. Death is instant. Some people use the pressure of a
thumb between the vertebrae to aid the dislocation.

The chin-up is a variation of the neck-pull. Hold on to the back legs
with one hand. Twist your other hand around its neck so that your thumb
is just behind the back of the head, your palm around the cheek, and your
finger under the chin. Stretch the rabbit and at the same time push its
chin backwards and upwards.

An alternative method is the karate chop but unless you are an expert
it can take several attempts to be effective, which is hardly humane or
efficient. The chop is a swift, sharp blow at the base of the rabbit's skull
with the side of your hand. A really forceful and accurate blow should kill
instantly (and can be done while the rabbit is still in the net) but you are

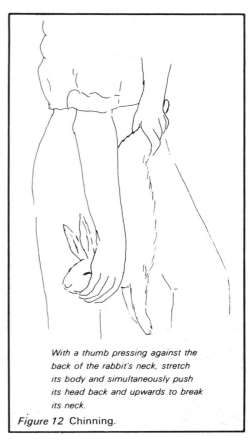

With a thumb pressing against the back of the rabbit's neck, stretch its body and simultaneously push its head back and upwards to break its neck.

Figure 12 Chinning.

more likely to stun the animal momentarily or knock it unconscious. If you cannot kill with one sharp blow, do not use this method.

Killing down and lying up

The aim of ferreting is to take rabbits for yourself, above ground, not to have the ferrets killing or wounding them underground and wasting the meat.

When the feel of the day is such that the rabbits are not in the mood to bolt, it is easier for the ferrets to kill down than to chase them out. But give them plenty of time to work the bury. Use your ears. If you hear a rabbit drumming, then a ferret is getting close to it. If you hear a rabbit squealing, it could mean a kill. Suspect that possibility if there is still no sign of the ferret twenty or thirty minutes later.

With several ferrets in action there is more chance of a rabbit being trapped between them, and a ferret might come up with blood on it or with rabbit fur (fleck) on its claws. Then there may be a dead rabbit in the tunnels or at least a rabbit stuck up a dead end and scrabbled at from the rear by a frustrated ferret.

There is no need to panic because you have not seen a loose ferret for quarter of an hour! Put your ear to the hole: you can learn so much by listening. If a rabbit is backed up in a dead end, you should be able to recognize the sound of a scrabbling ferret worrying at it. Try one or two tricks to bring out the ferret. Rattle a stick at the mouth of the hole, or make a back-of-the-hand squeak, and innate curiosity might bring the hunter up before it settles down in earnest. If you are ready to move on anyway, use your stick more vigorously to imitate a thumping rabbit, or stamp about a bit. Of course, even if the ferret comes up, the dead or injured rabbit will remain underground, and for the sake of humanity you do not want to leave an injured rabbit dying a lingering death in the bury. Once the ferret is up, you can use a length of bramble down the hole to locate a kill – wiggle it down the run, make contact, withdraw the bramble to see if it has rabbit fleck on it. Sometimes you can even hook out the rabbit itself this way but be very careful with this trick if any ferrets are still down below – it is not unknown for a ferret's back to be broken in such a manoeuvre. You cannot see what you have hooked.

If your ferret fails to respond to your squeaks and rattles, it is probably lying up, which is to say that it has settled in for a meal and maybe a good doze. Some lie-ups only last ten minutes and you would not be aware of them until your ferret shows up with blood on its face. Some lie-ups last an hour or more and if you have enough patience you can sit it out, with repeated enticements to encourage the ferret to emerge. Lying up is more likely as the day wears on and the ferret grows tired or hungry. Every ferret should have an hour's rest now and then, with a drink and a snack. The best bolting is often in the morning anyway, and if you call it a day by mid-afternoon you are less likely to need your graft.

If you want that rabbit for yourself, and if you do not have the time or patience to wait for a laid-up ferret, you will have to take active steps to retrieve them both.

Using the liner

The traditional way of retrieving is to send in a liner. The liner hob is friend to no ferret. He is at least a bully, if not a butcher. His job is to make a laid-up ferret get out fast, no questions asked, leaving the liner to stay on the kill while you dig down quickly before he can eat it.

A big liner coming up behind a busy little jill scrabbling at the back end of a rabbit hunched up in a dead end could give the jill a nip or two before she has a chance to move out, so take care and use your liner sparingly.

Once the guilty ferret is out and the liner has come to a halt, you can use a combination of hearing, intuition and basic engineering to locate the kill. If you have yard-marked the line, you will have some idea of how far in the liner is. Buries do not run in convenient straight lines, however: they meander, they go round and under obstacles, they link in with cross-tunnels and T-junctions, they go up blind alleys, they are on several levels. Follow the line as far as you can; use a hazel rod to test for turnings and junctions, and do a test dig at every possible change of direction to see which way the line goes next. But do not dig if any other ferrets are still down, because you might block their exit or even bury them unwittingly.

If you have marked the line at arm's length, you will be able to avoid ramming the graft blade straight into your liner's skull and you can dig carefully a yard away from him. You may have trouble in persuading him to part with his rabbit and in fact you should not try to do so while he is in the bury – it is his *job* to stay with the kill.

Ferreting poachers used a line on all their ferrets. They were trained to come out quick as soon as the line was tugged so that man and ferret could make a rapid departure when circumstances so demanded.

To dig or not

Digging should be a last resort, not only because it is hard work but also because too much digging will ruin the bury for later ferreting sessions. Some people do not dig on principle and try not to use ferrets that have any tendency to lie up. If they do have a lie-up, they prefer to call it a day – which they probably should have done earlier, before the ferret became bored, tired or hungry. In such a case you can try thumping, calling and whistling; the ferret might come to see what all the fuss is about if he has nothing better to do. If you have not got the time to sit around waiting, block up all the holes so that you can return later. By then your ferret should have slept off its meal and be quite pleased to see you. It is unlikely to dig its own way out overnight and if you thump at a hole and call in the early morning it will soon emerge, blinking sleepily, ferret fashion. Sleeping ferrets always take a lot of waking.

Better still, block up all the holes except the one where you last saw the ferret and leave a familiar carrying box there with a good bit of bedding, a drink of water (essential) and a tasty morsel. If you cannot spare a box, a comfortable bed of hay might do the trick. When you come back early next morning the ferret should be curled up on the bedding, sound asleep.

Make it early, though, before the ferret wanders off in search of another meal or a drink.

If by chance the ferret is not there when you return, keep checking for a least a week. It is likely to remain in the same area, but it is most unlikely to find its own way home even if you live only a field away. Your ferret will still be tame enough a week after you lost it, but the longer it is feral the wilder it will become until its reaction will be to flee and hide or, if cornered, to raise its hackles, fluff its tail, chatter furiously and spit like an angry cat. And it means it. You will have to tame it again gradually when you get home (food works wonders) and it may ever after be just that much spunkier than it was before it had a taste of self-sufficiency. Ferrets have been domesticated for centuries but the wildness of the polecat still lingers a little in their blood. If it did not, no escaped ferret could last as long as a week on its own.

Dealing with a rabbit carcase

Thumbing   When there is a lull in the action, 'thumb' the dead rabbit to empty its bladder – and be careful where you aim. Use one hand to hold the animal behind the shoulders and slide your other hand down the body towards the scut, using the pressure of your thumb along the belly and groin to squeeze out the urine.

Legging   Leg your rabbit by making a slit between the tendon and bone on one hind leg and pushing the other back foot through it. Make a nick at the back of the second ankle so that it does not slip out again. Then the rabbit can be hung head down on a handy branch or fence, or over your finger or pole when you carry it home. Hanging the rabbit head down while it is still warm will improve the meat by bleeding it.

Rabbits hang comfortably in pairs if you slot the second rabbit's hind-legs through those of the first. Leave one animal hanging on either side of the nearest fence, then collect up all your pairs at the end of the session rather than lugging them with you wherever you go.

Paunching   Gutting a warm rabbit is a messy job and you should leave it in a cool, shaded spot until it is cold. Then carefully insert the point of your knife into the belly so that you only just puncture the skin with a very small incision. Instead of slitting with the knife and risking penetration of the guts, insert your fingers and open the cavity by pulling equally from either side. Hook out the intestines all in one dollop – they should fall away easily from the rib cage. In warm weather make the slit as small as possible so that less meat is exposed and spoiled.

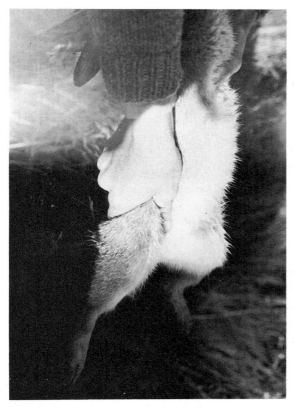

ABOVE: Thumbing: use your thumb to express the dead rabbit's urine. RIGHT: Legging: make a slit in one hind leg between tendon and bone, then push the other hind foot through the slit and nick it above the heel to secure it. Hang rabbits on a pole for easier carrying.

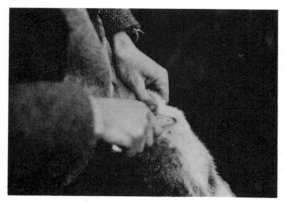

Paunching
1 Make a small slit in the fur with the tip of the knife.

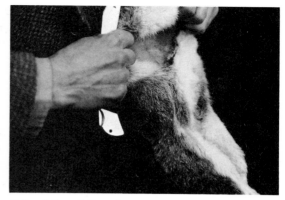

2 Carefully pull the pelt apart.

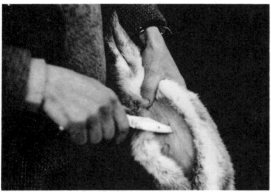

3 Slip the point of the knife through the skin, without puncturing any of the internal organs.

4 Gently ease your fingers into the slit.

5 Enlarge the opening by pulling it apart.

6 The guts will come out in one go.

If you forgot to thumb the rabbit before paunching, your knife might pierce the bladder and the meat will be tainted. If your knife punctures the guts, the job will be smelly as well as messy. Watch out for the gall bladder – if the gall is spilled the taint is very bitter, unpleasant and persistent.

Clearing up

At the end of the session gather up all your nets and count them in; give your ferrets another good drink and dry their feet carefully if they are wet and muddy; tidy up any digging; pick up all your gear and rubbish; hang your legged rabbits on a pole over your shoulder; drop a brace off at the farmhouse or let the keeper know you are off and thank him for a good day. You might only have one rabbit to take home, or even none; you might have cursed and sweated over difficult digging; you might ... well, a lot of things might or might not have happened, but once you have been ferreting you will always want to go again, if only for the joy of working as a team with an animal for catching food – an animal that you cannot help but admire for its intelligence, skill, courage, tenacity and character. Look after it well.

Shooting to ferrets

Shooting almost destroys the point of ferreting, which should be to take a few clean rabbits for the table. Ferreting is not an efficient way of controlling the rabbit population; shooting is not the best way of catching a meal, and it does entail a degree of risk to the ferret if one of the guns is overhasty. You can, of course, dispense with purse nets and shoot rabbits as they bolt, with or without the back-up of long nets or dogs, but this book does not intend to teach you how to shoot. There are plenty of books specializing in that subject.

RATS

If you care for your ferrets, you will not use them for ratting. However fast and brave a ferret is, the time comes when she (jills are usually used for ratting) will get viciously bitten by a cornered rat.

However, rats have always feared ferrets and ferrets have always been employed as ratters. Sportsmen have always enjoyed using them, and you are more likely to be given permission to ferret rats than rabbits. Farmers are only too pleased to get rid of a few rats, especially if they are in a corner of the farm where you and your ferrets and terriers are not likely to cause any harm to anything other than the rats.

You still need to remember that, even if you think you are doing the farmer a favour, it is a privilege to be granted access to his land for ferreting. If you intend to use dogs, make it quite clear in your negotiations for the privilege and do not sneak them in unless he has specifically said that you can. The same applies to guns, of course, only more so.

Fix up a day and time with the farmer and, to quote Wessex Ferret Club's 'Stoat': 'On the day, bloody well be there! Try to spot him or his wife, call a cheery "hello", say something about "just off to the pit" in case the old dog's forgotten all about you already ... Enjoy your work ... and when you've done, let him know and ask if you may return. Never make a nuisance of yourself and try to be regular in your comings and goings. In time you'll come to know each other better and that's when, during a chat over the gate, he may just ask you "Why don't you bring a terrier along?" or perhaps even (wait for it!) "Have a go at those damned rabbits up on the top field." Er, just make sure that you've offered to help muck out the sheds before then, and have done it well too.'

For ratting you need very active and lively ferrets, small enough to run about easily down the rat holes (so likely to be jills) but fierce enough to win in a fight if there is one. Rats, given the option, would always rather flee a ferret than fight it but they may not have that option.

You also need a wholly reliable terrier that has been brought up with the ferrets and knows them very well indeed, so that they can work as a team with the ferrets bolting the rats and the dog killing the rats but never mistaking a ferret for a rat in the heat of the moment. A good ratting ferret is the 'greyhound' or 'lurcher' type: long, thin, and very fast indeed – an ideal poacher's ferret!

If a ferret shows any reluctance for ratting, never push it: you will end up with a mangled ferret. If you do go ratting it is essential to have your ferrets properly vaccinated beforehand. And if they do get bitten, take them straight to the vet. Do not mess about with your own cures. It is not worth the risk.

A final caution on rats from Wessex's 'Stoat', who writes graphically of his experiences and who can laugh at himself in even the direst circumstances: 'Went rat catching. Big expert at this game! Regular little Brian Plummer! Killed a few. Used to take them home in a satchel – not sure why, in matured retrospect. Long hot days. Ferrets, shotguns, biscuits, I'd take the lot. Took something one day I hadn't bargained on! Get this: Rich Tea fingers. In the satchel, right? Few dead rats? Yep! Pop them in! Hungry? Why, then eat a biscuit, Stanley. There's me eating biscuits literally from under dead bloody rats! Know how dead animals tend to leak a little bit of pee? Ever heard of Wiels Disease? (sic?). I bloody soon did! Blame went everywhere! Dad killed my polecat. Mum burnt the

badger skin I was working on. Me? Bloody near died! My fault! I've learnt.'

There are lots more stories where that one came from!

HAWKS AND THINGS

There are those who ferret to hawks, which is an exciting combination and which makes the most of two natural and admirable predators (three if you count Man) working as a team. There are those who hire out their ferrets to companies and corporations that want a liner to take something through a pipe or a conduit. There are those who turn their ferrets into fur pelts, a subject which needs a separate book. There are those who simply enjoy their ferrets as pets – and we have written a special chapter for them.

There is a lot you can do with a ferret.

9 Bag and Pot

There you are, striding home with a hard-earned bag of rabbits. You have already given the livers to the ferrets as a token of gratitude. What next? There is plenty you can do with rabbits.

You can sell them. There is usually a market for good clean rabbits, and ferreted rabbits fetch a much better price than shot ones. Only sell the best: get a reputation for quality. To have some idea of a rabbit's age and corresponding toughness, press its jawbones together. If they crack it is a tender rabbit, so mark it up for sale. Other indications of youth and tenderness are smooth sharp claws, easily torn and delicate ears, small white teeth, a narrow cleft in the jaw and a short neck. Doe rabbits are more tender than bucks and they can be identified by their narrow heads as well as by genitals. A big old buck is the toughest meat of the lot.

Before you start ferreting with a view to selling your rabbits, check the market carefully. The usual outlets are game dealers and butchers. Some dealers want the innards left intact because they export them to make things like pâté. Some want the carcase fresh, paunched and skinned. Some prefer a whole frozen rabbit, skin and all, and you can fill up your freezer and take them along when there are enough to make the journey worthwhile. Rabbit meat is in season from September to March and considered to be at its best from October to February.

But most of all you will be ferreting for your own pot. The first step, assuming you thumbed and paunched in the field, is to skin the rabbit, but if you plan to find a use for its pelt you should skin *before* you paunch. Like this:

1 Make slits in both hind feet and hang the rabbit from two meat-hooks, separated by a bar to keep the hind legs well apart.

2 Slit the skin carefully right around the neck, just behind the chin line for maximum pelt, and then sever the head by cutting through the neck cartilage.

3 Slit the skin (and only the skin) on each back leg as if you were making ankle-length boots – as close to the heel as possible – and then make a long slit from ankle to ankle along the inner thighs, around the genitals and anus and over the upper side of the scut.

4 Cut off the front paws.

5 Carefully loosen the skin on the back legs and pull the whole pelt evenly down the body and off over the severed neck. Your pelt is a complete tube. Now you can gut the carcase as usual.

There is a market for pelts if you know where to find it, and all you have to do is pack the pelts in pairs, separated by brown paper. There is no need to cure them in any way.

If you are only interested in the meat, paunch in the field and skin at home. A good dose of pepper will keep flies away if you hang the un-skinned rabbit in a shed, but, unlike some game, rabbit is not usually hung. When you are ready, chop off the rabbit's head and all four feet at the first joint, loosen the skin along the paunching slit, take it over the hind legs then strip it off over the front end. If it is a tender rabbit, the skin will come off easily. Tough skinning, tough rabbit.

An even quicker way of skinning is to slice the pelt in half around the middle and slip it off like a pair of trousers and a pullover.

Your ferrets will appreciate the head if it is still fresh. Some people, however, leave the head on if they are cooking the rabbit whole, which makes skinning a more delicate operation, especially as the skinned ears are left on for the sake of appearances. The eyes are removed before cooking. The carcase is then trussed, with the head raised up and pushed back between the shoulders.

Drop the skinned carcase into cold water with a large pinch of salt. Soak it for an hour to whiten the meat and make the flavour more delicate, then dry it well. Some people prefer to pour boiling water over it instead. If the meat is tainted try washing it in diluted vinegar.

You can cook your rabbit whole or you can butcher it into four 'wings and thighs', two back pieces, two rib sections and a meaty saddle or loin.

A really tender young rabbit can be fried like chicken pieces. A slightly less tender one can be baked or roasted, but if you have any doubts about tenderness you should stew it.

The average weight before baking is about three pounds and this reduces to just under two pounds of meat after it has been cooked and the bones and other waste have been discarded.

To keep a baked or roasted rabbit nice and juicy you can stuff it. Elizabeth Craig suggests using a mixture of oatmeal, onion, sage and suet; or sausage meat; or veal stuffing mixed with chopped liver, heart and kidneys. Ann Kanable, who farms domestic rabbits in the United States, prefers a chopped vegetable stuffing of onions, carrots, cooked lima beans, peas, celery, potato and green pepper. Give it plenty of dripping and baste it frequently during the roasting. You could lay a few strips of bacon on the rabbit to keep it moist.

Make gravy in the usual way from the juices and add stewed tomatoes to it. Serve roast rabbit with the gravy, bread sauce and bacon.

Onion sauce and fried bacon go well with boiled rabbit. Simmer it gently until it is tender, with vegetables, bouquet garni, peppercorns and salt. Use the stock for soup.

You can do a lot more with a rabbit than just boil or roast it. Modern cookery books hardly mention rabbit at all, but the pre-myxy books are full of imaginative and delicious recipes. For example, the jointed meat is good curried (served with boiled rice, slices of lemon and grated coconut) or stewed with vegetables and savoury dumplings or in cider. Dear old Mrs Beeton gives recipes galore – fricassee, casserole, ragout, pilau, assorted stews, ways with 'cutlets, darioles and fillets' (darioles involve pounded rabbit, mushrooms, oysters and celery), fried rabbit in breadcrumbs served with tartare sauce, jugged rabbit, marbled rabbit (a marvellous moulded dish involving pickled pork, forcemeat balls, liver, kidney, sliced eggs and sliced rabbit all decoratively layered in gelatine), rabbit in aspic, rabbit pies, puddings and patties, braised and larded rabbit, rabbit stewed in milk, rabbit for invalids, rabbit cream (minced rabbit combined with white sauce and steamed in a mould) and rabbit soufflé.

Ann Kanable gives some more up-to-date ideas for rabbit and biscuit pie, rabbit sandwich spread, rabbit salads, creole rabbit (in a rich sauce based on garlic, tomato juice and Worcester sauce), rabbit with tortillas, and fried battered livers and hearts.

Mrs K. Bridges, a cook familiar to television viewers of *Upstairs Downstairs*, said in her original *Practical Household Cookery* (published in 1905) that the Wiltshire estate's warrener used to ferret for rabbits and that her Rabbit Pie was very popular with the staff – not surprisingly as it included claret!

Several of the older books give variations of Indian rabbit, rabbit brawn and paste, harvest rabbit and gipsy pie. Here are some of them, culled (with permission) from *Farmers Weekly*'s collection of recipes sent in by 'country housewives' from all over Britain in the late 1940s, when rabbits were appreciated.

INDIAN RABBIT
For 4–5 persons:

1 rabbit	1 onion
3 tbspn fresh or	1 tbspn curry powder
desiccated coconut	4 tbspn butter or margarine
½ cup milk	1 tspn sugar
1 cup gravy or stock	1 tspn salt

Joint the rabbit and fry to a light brown in smoking hot butter. Remove from pan. Fry chopped onion lightly. Add curry powder, coconut, sugar, salt, milk and stock. Return joints to pan and simmer for an hour. Pile up hot boiled rice in centre of a hot dish and encircle with rabbit masked with sauce. Serve with chutney.

GIPSY PIE

1 tender rabbit	4 oz (100 g) cooked ham or pork sausages
8 oz (225 g) beef steak	Salt, pepper, nutmeg
2 tspn chopped parsley	Stock
8 oz (225 g) flaky pastry	

Soak rabbit in cold salted water for an hour and a half. Wipe dry, joint. Slice ham, or skin sausages, and with floured hands make meat into round balls. Cut steak into small pieces. Arrange rabbit, ham or balls and beef in pie dish. Sprinkle over the parsley, grated nutmeg, pepper, salt to taste. Add stock, cover with pastry, bake slowly for 1½ hours after the pastry has risen.

RABBIT PASTE

1 rabbit	Lump of margarine the size of an egg
1 lump of sugar	12 allspice
6 peppercorns	3 blades mace
1 onion stuck with 12 cloves	

Cut rabbit into small joints and put in casserole with other ingredients. Cover closely and cook slowly until the meat leaves the bones easily. When cold put the meat through a mincer two or three times, then beat together with 8 oz (225 g) margarine or butter, 1 dspnfl Worcester sauce, a little cayenne and a teaspoon of sugar. Put into small pots and pour over a little melted butter or margarine.

PELTS

Home curing is suitable for knick-knacks but something like a jacket needs professionally tanned skins if it is to be serviceable. Here are four home-curing methods, starting with the simplest.

1 Just pin the skin, furside inwards, to a shed wall and let it dry. It will not be good for much!

2 Rub lots of ordinary salt into the inside surface of a fresh skin, spread it out, anchor it flat and leave it to dry in a cool, airy place out of the sun for three or four days. Then scrape off any dried fat etc. It is a little better than just drying it.

3 Use a 50/50 mixture of salt and alum in the above process. When the skin is dry, peel off any fatty tissue, wash the skin very gently in mild

soap, rinse well without wringing, hang out to dry in the shade for a couple of days and then rub it, fur side down, over a clothes-line a few times. Work in a softener like saddle soap or neatsfoot oil to make it pliable.

4 Soak in constantly tepid water (change it frequently) for three hours. Scrape off all fat. Rinse. Wipe with a little white spirit to remove the last traces of grease, dirt and stains. Make up two pints of water and dissolve 4 oz of alum in it. Make up a separate solution of 1 oz washing soda and 2 oz salt in one pint of water, then add in the alum solution, stirring well. Stir a little water into some plain flour and work it into a thick paste with the alum/salt/soda liquid. Pin out the skin and paste it (avoiding the fur itself). Leave it for 24 hours, scrape off the old paste, coat it again, leave for another 24 hours, scrape, paste for the third and last time and leave for three more days before scraping. Then rinse in water containing an ounce of borax to the gallon; rinse completely in clean tepid water. Squeeze without wringing, pull into shape, pin on a clean board fur side down, paint all over with neatsfoot oil and leave to dry. Then work it fur side down over a bar until it is supple. Put it in a shallow container and cover it with sawdust (hardwood, not softwood). Work the sawdust into it, then hang it out to dry completely.

More ambitious still? There are several books devoted to curing skins, taxidermy and allied arts.

10   Pets and Characters

Ferrets can make delightfully friendly and entertaining pets. They are still unusual enough in this context to attract enquiring or wary glances. Many people would not recognize a ferret if they saw one, and if they did recognize it they would probably come out with the standard, prejudiced, half-joking and half-serious remarks about nasty things that bite and stink.

At a recent Game Fair the ferret stand drew a good crowd. A television team entered the enclosure, the cameraman uncomfortably aware of the ferrets that scampered near his ankles. Newspaper photographers tried to persuade ferrets to keep still for more than half a second as they perched on someone's hat or around a friendly neck. Young lads leaned over the barriers, eager to befriend one of the small animals. Grown men stood around in smug silence with grins on their faces: they knew all about ferrets, they had worked them when they were lads and they had many a tale to tell. No, mate, they were not going to handle an unknown ferret – oh no!

The children, who often have a natural understanding of animals (unless they have been taught to fear them by their parents), were intrigued by the sight of a score of ferrets, of all sizes, ages and colours, frolicking in the enclosure. Shallow trenches criss-crossed the area, covered with glass so that the 'underground' games could be watched by the onlookers. It

Young ferrets at the Game Fair.

was a hot day – bad weather for ferrets – and as the morning wore on the animals took refuge in shady corners provided under cut branches and boards, where they sprawled in tangles for a nap. Even as they dozed, they fascinated the children who enjoyed their abandoned sleeping positions and their habit of lying all over each other with no ferret protesting at being bottom of the heap.

The women looked on warily, trying to ignore childish requests of 'Can't we have a ferret, mum?' We took out a few of the animals and offered them to the women to hold. Under friendly encouragement, they accepted gingerly and their attitudes changed completely. 'They're lovely! Their fur's all soft!' said one, stroking an inquisitive young jill who was as interested in the woman as the woman was in the animal. Soon everyone wanted to stroke a ferret and mothers were saying to their children, 'Well, we might *think* about having one,' as they queued to learn more about these captivating animals which had turned out to be nothing like the stinking biting creatures of legend.

They were right to think before deciding. You will have realized from the rest of this book that there is more to keeping ferrets than there is to pet mice or budgies. They are animals that deserve your full respect but with knowledgeable care they can offer you a great deal in return. Please do not acquire ferrets on an impulse – and please read the whole of this book while you are considering the possibilities of keeping them. Be

Pet ferrets get into the unlikeliest places . . .

warned that people who do have pet ferrets get addicted to them, and be warned, too, that as with any animal it is the owner that makes a good or bad pet. If you are afraid of ferrets, you have no right to keep one as a pet; they are sensitive to your reactions and they need to be trusted and loved.

Ferrets have many characteristics that are good qualities in a pet. They are small animals – smaller than cats – and they do not need much living space at all. A minor disadvantage of their size is that they can get underfoot without being noticed and, naturally, react with some annoyance if they are trodden on. A shod foot can cause considerable damage to something as small as a ferret.

They have very clean habits and will always mess in the same place, which makes house-training to a litter tray very simple. Most of them cause no damage inside the house – although we do know of at least one character who could wreak havoc if he suspected there were housemice around the place. The fact that a ferret is in residence, by the way, is likely to deter housemice and rats from moving in, and in some parts of the world domestic ferrets have always been kept as house animals to control such pests.

Ferrets are portable, too. You can pop them into a small carrier or your pocket. Wendy Winsted, the American author of a book about pet ferrets, takes her pets with her when she rides on public transport and they sit happily on her lap or in her bag, readily accepting the hesitant caresses of complete strangers. In London, too, girls have been seen with their pet ferrets prancing along beside them on leads in the park. In the country valley where this book is being written a young girl is often seen in the lanes with a poley on one lead and a massive mongrel of Dobermann pinscher extraction on another. Ferrets can get on well with other household animals, particularly cats. We know of people who keep domestic rabbits, chickens and mice as well as ferrets, but they are never foolish enough to test the ferret's benevolence towards its natural prey and they fully appreciate the importance of keeping their ferrets securely housed.

We have met pet owners who keep their ferrets in outdoor hutches with garden exercise runs, and those who keep their ferrets loose in the house like any cat or dog. There are a few drawbacks to loose living: ferrets can get themselves into the most unlikely places and their owners might find them curled up in the oven or the washing machine – imagine the possible consequences! One very pregnant jill, who had long ago selected an inaccessible place behind the kitchen boiler as her latrine, decided categorically that she would nest in an underwear drawer, where she successfully raised a beautiful litter to the consternation of the daughter whose underwear occupied the drawer. (Naturally the daughter was the one member of the

family who had never really liked ferrets.) The jill, Flo, insisted on dragging various members of the family to look at the brand-new kits, in sharp contrast to those jills that will kill their kits if anyone goes near them. Other pet owners have similar stories of being invited to inspect a new litter, and it might be that the jills are treating their keepers like kits and trying to pull them into the nest for safety!

Most pet ferrets, if properly handled from a very young age, are loving and affectionate to their owners, but care should be taken in the breeding season, particularly with uncastrated hobs. If you take the trouble to spend a lot of time with your animal you will be able to read his moods. Nobby was a particularly intelligent and friendly hob, described by his keeper as 'soft and loving', but as his breeding season progressed he tended to become increasingly edgy and frustrated, even if he had mated. His aggression towards men was noticeable and even the most familiar man had to make a point of dominating him, sometimes quite roughly. The hob had to know his limits.

Nobby bit his owner once, as a reprimand, and she takes full blame on herself for failing to read the warning message he had given her. Much more typically, Nobby loved nothing more than lying on his back in a drowsy state, having his tummy rubbed, while he yawned with a paw to his mouth – very human, and very ferret.

Jackie Spencer's pet hob, C.B., also enjoys a relaxed doze on anyone's lap. Jackie has kept several ferrets for several years and is one of those who has been privileged to monitor the progress of litters from the day they

OPPOSITE LEFT: C.B. The lap ferret.   CENTRE: Happy families.   RIGHT: Gardening ferret, complete with harness.

were born. C.B. stands for 'Cry Baby', of all things – he happened to be the noisiest kit in the litter. Mike Jasper's enormous hob, who is a television star in his own right, is called Cuddles, while its timid, shy companion hobble is known affectionately as Killer.

It is very important that you should understand your ferret. For everyone's sake do not keep ferrets if you have very young children. A ferret has more of a sense of dignity than most dogs; it will not tolerate a toddler's teasing, and it may not be immediately friendly towards strangers. However, a ferret is an excellent pet for a child old enough to accept responsibility for it, and keeping a ferret is a very good way of learning a lot about such responsibilities. Too many mothers (for some reason it is usually mothers rather than fathers who object to pet ferrets) have deprived their children of the joy and valuable experience of caring for a ferret.

Although wild polecats are on the whole solitary animals, and although many a ferret has been a young boy's sole companion, living with him every moment of the day, snuggled into his pocket wherever he goes, it is fairer to the ferret to keep it with another of its kind. Ferrets enjoy each other's company. They are very playful, full of curiosity and energy. They are also quite fearless, and will poke their noses into electric fires and real fires, so have a care. They have a strong instinct to hoard things – and not just for food. Small items like shiny objects or even the odd sock might be discovered hidden under the armchair or behind the fridge. They also hide themselves, curling up in any dark corner for a snooze, so they are easily shut in a room or a cupboard or drawer by mistake.

Pet ferrets are an affectionate lot and they will often indicate that they want to be picked up for a tickle, responding with a chuckle of pleasure to a favourite caress. Apart from chuckling, and chattering when they are excited, they are pleasantly quiet animals and will not disturb the neighbours.

Many a pet ferret helps its owner with the gardening, but do be careful that it does not wander off unnoticed. A jill on heat, however home-loving, might well mooch off in search of a mate, or a pregnant jill might go on a hunt for a suitable nesting place down some rabbit hole. Ferrets can squeeze through the unlikeliest gaps, remember, and very few gardens are ferret-proof.

Housing a house pet is simple. It needs a litter box for a latrine, a regular eating place (watch out for bits of food being stored away in inaccessible corners), a constant source of fresh drinking-water and a dark cosy place to sleep in, like a well-bedded cardboard box. Wild polecats are crepuscular rather than nocturnal (they are at their most active at dusk and dawn) but ferrets have largely adapted to the human routines that govern their domesticated lives. They are expert nappers and can drop off to sleep in seconds. In the daytime they can take quite a lot of waking – they sleep as deeply as a man with a clear conscience and even at feeding time might take some rousing. In their own time they will emerge from their sleeping hole, blinking in the bright light, yawning, scratching and peering up at you to enquire what all the fuss is about.

Central heating is not very good for ferrets. We have already talked about possible breeding problems in a hot environment, and a centrally heated house also might not do wonders for a ferret's coat.

The general principles of ferret care outlined in the rest of this book apply also to pet ferrets. Outside accommodation can be adapted from any of the systems we have described, and some of the luckiest ferrets we have met had an indoor two-room cage (living room and dark sleeping box) with a cat-flap out into their own private garden enclosure, so that they could come and go as they pleased. They also had regular play sessions with their owner and went for a daily walk on leads with harnesses. Harnesses are much safer than collars; for one thing any ferret can slip its collar easily enough (its slim head is no obstruction), but on the other hand if a collared ferret does escape it runs the risk of catching its collar and either throttling or trapping itself. Harnesses are more comfortable as well as safer and you should be able to buy a suitable cat harness from a petshop.

Some pet owners are concerned about the smell of a ferret. All animals smell, including humans. The well-kept and properly fed ferret has a faint musk which many people find attractive rather than unpleasant. Uncastrated hobs in the breeding season will smell rather stronger. It is possible to remove the anal glands that are responsible for much of this smell, but you should consult your veterinary surgeon and weigh his advice very carefully. Plenty of vets are not happy to 'de-scent' an animal, for ethical reasons, as we discuss in Chapter 6. Some people bath their ferrets but this is not really necessary if you keep your pet's accommodation spotlessly clean and feed it properly. Most ferrets do not enjoy the indignity of a bath – they do not even enjoy a voluntary dip in hot weather, although some like playing with a jet from a hosepipe. Some like being groomed gently with a soft brush, but some do not.

If you have jills, it is essential to consult your vet about the possibility of spaying. De-scenting is an operation normally performed for the sake of the owner rather than the ferret, but spaying is often very much in the interests of the jill because of the potential problems of prolonged oestrus and the possible long-term effects of hormone treatment.

Your pet ferret is a character and will quickly become important to you. You will naturally turn to your vet for advice when necessary and we strongly urge you to be on good terms with him and to consult him too soon rather than too late. If you notice any unusual behaviour or condition, talk to the vet as soon as possible. If you cannot afford private veterinary fees, you can seek the advice of the People's Dispensary for Sick Animals (PDSA) who maintain more than sixty animal treatment centres in England, Scotland, Wales and overseas and who offer free advice and treatment for sick and injured animals.

However, ferrets kept in good conditions are rarely ill. The most likely ailments are abscesses arising from wounds of one kind or another, colds or 'flu caught from you, or occasional problems with ear mites, fleas, ticks and so on if the quarters are not kept clean. Your vet can prescribe appropriate remedies, much the same as he would for a pet dog or cat.

Playing is very ferret and there are many ways of keeping a pet entertained. Cardboard tubes, boxes and paper bags will be explored indefatigably and used for ambushes. Ping-pong balls and eggs provide endless amusement. A pile of logs or just a loose stack of paper or rags gives scope for investigation. Anything dangling on a string can be batted about, in the way that a kitten does (and even the most mature ferret normally behaves just like a kitten). Bones can be chewed or hidden. If you are generous with space and your time, make a big outdoor enclosure with lots of branches to clamber on, artificial tunnels to explore, scrape-holes to be

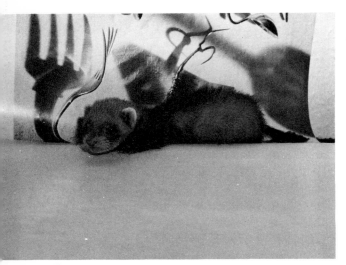

Ferrets are tough.

Posers.

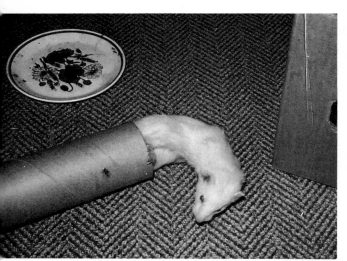

Tubes and boxes provide endless entertainment.

There is something about ferrets!

excavated (as long as they don't lead to the way out!) and anything else your imagination runs to if you think ferret.

Enjoy a romp with your ferret, give it plenty of affection and attention, and best of all give it the company of other ferrets for playing, snuggling together, bickering, gossiping and general sociability. Pet ferrets have a great deal to offer the caring owner, and they *deserve* caring owners. There is something about ferrets and it is a privilege to know them.

PART II

Vet Check * Ferret Facts * Nutrition Tables * Glossary
Useful Addresses * Bibliography and References * Index

Vet Check

INTRODUCTION

This section was devised in consultation with a number of veterinary surgeons and others with experience of the ferret, particularly John Cooper, Nicholas Mills, John Knight, Dominic Wells, Michael Oxenham, Alan Mowlem and Dr John Hammond Jr.

There are several reasons why vets may not be familiar with ferrets. The animals tend to mask clinical signs (like many wild creatures) so that sudden death, apparently without cause, is quite a common phenomenon. Even in less dramatic cases ferret owners have traditionally consulted each other rather than the profession and tend to be wary of paying veterinary fees on behalf of an animal which may have been acquired for only a couple of pounds.

Although ferrets have been domesticated for many centuries, and have more recently performed an invaluable role as laboratory animals, there is still considerable controversy about the species and many areas of ignorance. The situation is improving quite rapidly, especially since ferrets are increasingly popular as pets (particularly in the United States) and, perhaps more to the encouragement of research into their problems, their value as fur-bearing animals has been recognized in New Zealand. There the Ministry of Agriculture has begun to draw together any material of value to fitch farmers and has been most helpful in supplying details of reported disorders and treatments.

Ferret Facts at the end of this section gives much of the basic data about the species. Vet Check is intended to offer guidance on handling, diagnosis and treatment, but it *is* for guidance only and professional judgment is of course essential.

Our Bibliography (p. 179) includes some useful technical references but it is a very abbreviated list of the available material. A great deal has been written about the ferret, particularly in a laboratory situation (which is not necessarily of direct practical value to vets and ferret owners) and a full bibliography would be a book in itself. We have many hundreds of references on file and there are many more available through the Commonwealth Bureau of Animal Health's computer records. We also have details of products which have been used successfully in treating ferrets, but very few are actually licensed for them and we have therefore not been able to publish many trade names in this book, although the pharmaceutical companies have responded generously to our requests for information.

HANDLING

Despite prejudiced rumours to the contrary, most ferrets are friendly, playful and attractive animals by nature. If they are not, it is more likely to be the fault of the owner than the ferret.

Most ferrets are amenable to handling and will not bite if approached sensibly. Be confident and unhesitating in all your movements. Avoid using gloves unless the animal is genuinely bad-tempered or unused to being handled. Ask the *owner* to remove the ferret from its container: an alien hand plunging in may not be welcome. Let the ferret find its bearings, then offer it the back of your fist (never finger-tips) by way of introduction so that if it is inclined to bite little harm will be done. If you are not wholly confident, a little meat is a useful distraction while you inspect the ferret for fleas etc. An animal that is used to handling can be picked up gently with a hand under its chest.

To handle a doubtful animal, restrain it with one smooth movement (hesitancy imitates prey and invites biting) by holding it firmly above the shoulders, thumb and forefinger around the neck. If your thumb rests under the animal's chin it can be used to close its mouth; your other fingers can control the forelegs gently.

Ferrets are usually quite content to relax if suspended by such a hold, although hindquarter support is needed for gravid or obese animals. We do *not* recommend suspending the animal by its tail.

If there is a tendency to bite, you can press your knuckles into the ferret's mouth or flick a finger on its nose. When a ferret bites in earnest, its tendency as an efficient predator is to maintain its grip and no attempt should be made to pull away. Do not suspend the animal; it may let go if you place it on a flat surface, whereas a suspended animal will be loth to drop. The quickest release aid is a cold-water tap.

An alarmed or annoyed ferret will arch its back, fluff out its tail and chatter, although it can be difficult to recognize the difference between play attack and serious intent. Only if it is really frightened will it release its musk.

ADMINISTRATIONS

Injections

Subcutaneous: into the scruff. No assistant is needed. Use the finger and thumb to hold the animal around the neck with one hand while administering the injection with the other.

Intramuscular: posterior thigh muscle. If necessary, an assistant can wrap the ferret in a towel to restrain it.
Intraperitoneal: body cavity medial to hind leg.
Intravenous: no large superficial veins suitable for injection.

Oral

Most ferrets readily accept doses in milk or in food (chocolate seems to be favoured by some). Otherwise, hold the animal as described under Handling, so that it is in a vertical position. Use a non-chewable, non-puncturable dosing tube, syringe or glass dropper. Insert it at the side of the ferret's mouth behind its teeth and introduce the liquid gently on the back of its tongue. Tablets, pills and capsules can be introduced with a pair of long forceps or a plastic cat-type dispenser. To open the ferret's mouth, depress the lower jaw with a wooden spatula.

Nasal

An assistant should hold the ferret upright with its head tilted back. Use an inoculating sprayer to administer nasal doses.

Blood sampling

For samples of more than 0.5 ml, handling of a conscious ferret can be difficult and sedation should be used if necessary.
(i)   Toe-nail clipping (0.5 ml).
(ii) Tail vein: Shave underside of last two inches of tail, smear lightly with Vaseline. Incise vein at oblique angle with narrow scalpel blade.
(iii) Jugular vein: Sedation is usually necessary.

Temperature

Have the animal in a comfortable, relaxed position for rectal temperature check.

Toe-nail clipping

Either ask the owner to hold the animal, or wrap it in a towel and present one leg at a time.

ANAESTHETICS AND SEDATION

The following techniques have been used successfully in practice and laboratories. Inhalation anaesthetics mixed with oxygen are administered initially by open mask and then maintained by intubation. If injectable agents are used, an accurate weight to the nearest 20 g is essential. Premedication with ATROPINE (0.05 mg/kg subcut.) is needed with all agents except DOMITOR.

Gaseous anaesthetics:
   Isofluorane – gives quick induction at 4% and maintenance at 2%. Quick recovery.
   Halothane with nitrous oxide has been widely used but is being superseded by Isofluorane.
   Ether is very irritant to the respiratory system but has good margin of safety. Now largely superseded.

Injectable anaesthetic:
   Medetomidine (Domitor) 120 μg/kg given with *Ketamine* (Vetelar, Ketaset) 10 mg/kg, by intramuscular injection into the quadriceps muscle. Induction is very quick – about 1.5 minutes and gives anaesthesia for about 20 minutes. The antagonist for Domitor is Antisedan 0.5 mg/kg i/m.

Sedative agents:
   Ketamine (Vetelar, Ketaset) – 25 mg/kg i/m.
   Fentanyl/Fluanisone (Hypnorm) – 0.5 ml/kg i/m.
   Xylazine (Rompun) – 4 mg/kg subcut.
   Alphaxalone-alphadolone (Saffan) – 12 mg/kg i/m.

SURGICAL

Castration
Castration is recommended for pet hobs to reduce aggression and roaming tendencies. It reduces odour markedly and keeps albino coats white (they tend to become yellowy-orange through the activity of sebaceous glands in the whole male and in a sick animal). It is unlikely that castration will affect a ferret's working ability.
Age: 6–8 months. Techniques as for a small cat, or the 'dog closed' method. Note that the ferret is a photoperiodic breeder: in Britain enlargement of the testes may begin during late December on average and can be recognized at that stage by palpation. Full size is normally attained by the end of January and regression occurs as the male's season ends during July/August.

Spaying
Spaying is a simple procedure carrying little risk and is strongly advised for pet jills not required for breeding. The ferret is an induced ovulator and failure to curtail oestrus (by mating or other means) can give rise to many problems, some fatal.

Age: 6–8 months, during anoestrus or oestrus. Routine technique, midline incision. Note that a pad of fat can mask the ovaries of a ferret in good condition.

Vasectomy

Jill owners may find that a vasectomized hob is useful for bringing jills out of oestrus. However, this might increase the risk of pyometra and some owners prefer the hormonal 'jill jab'. The pseudopregnancy from mating with a vasectomized hob will last only 42–45 days and the procedure will then have to be repeated.

Anal glands

We do not advise removal of the musk-producing anal glands, although this is common practice in the United States on pet hobs and is carried out during castration. We consider such cosmetic treatment to be unnecessary mutilation, in the interests of the owner rather than the animal, and it has little effect on the ferret's natural odour. Removal of the glands may lead to prolapse of the anus unless correct procedures are followed carefully. The glands are used mainly for territorial scent-marking and sometimes for defence, and it should be borne in mind that ferrets are expert escapers. If gland excision is necessary in the interests of the animal the canine routine should be modified for ferrets (ref. Creed J.E., Kainer R.A. 'Surgical extirpation and related anatomy of anal sacs of the ferret', JAVMA 179: 575–7, 1981). Occasionally the glands become impacted and require emptying.

VACCINATION

Ferrets are highly susceptible to canine distemper, which is almost invariably fatal and is very infectious within a colony. Vaccination against this virus is recommended.

There is no substantiated evidence that ferrets are susceptible to leptospirosis, feline infectious enteritis, canine parvovirus, canine hepatitis, feline calicivirus or herpes virus or mink virus enteritis.

Canine distemper

Vaccination is given by the subcutaneous route. It is essential to avoid vaccines that are not sufficiently attenuated for ferret use, because the result will otherwise be fatal.

There is no distemper vaccine licensed for ferrets in the UK. Vaccine products are always changing and it is important for the veterinary surgeon to check with the manufacturer that their product is safe for ferrets.

Nobivac and Delcavac DHPPiL (Intervet) are licensed for use in the ferret in Scandinavia and are safe. The distemper fraction is from the Onderstepoort strain grown on the Vero cell line. The HPPiL fraction, although not needed, does not appear to harm the ferret. The first dose can be given from 12 weeks of age with a booster every 2 years.

For immediate immunity (lasting 2–3 weeks) in cases of known exposure, Maxaglobin (Hoechst) is licensed for use in ferrets: 0.2 mg/kg/ subcut or i/m.

Other vaccinations
It is possible to vaccinate against *rabies* (killed only – there are no rabies vaccines licensed for use in ferrets in the UK and it has recently been suggested that the ferret has only a low susceptibility to the virus), *influenza* (attenuated live virus gives 5 weeks immunity) and *C-type botulism* (commercial ferrets may need protection by inoculation at weaning with type C botulism toxoid, which will give one year's protection, but this should not be necessary for pet ferrets fed on fresh food).

The Fur Breeders Association imports and controls vaccine from the US and advises its members to vaccinate ferrets annually against distemper, botulism and enteritis.

JILLS AND LITTERS
The ferret is an induced ovulator and a photoperiodic breeder. An unmated jill will remain in season for several months from March to about September (at UK latitudes). Full details of photoperiodicity are discussed in various papers referred to in the Bibliography, and work continues on this theme.

Prolonged oestrus
It is possible to effect year-round breeding and encourage the production of several litters a year by adjusting day-length routines. In this respect it should be noted that pet ferrets kept indoors are often subjected to artificial lighting and that this has been known to induce oestrus as early as November.

The oestrous jill is easily recognized by her very swollen vulva and if she remains in oestrus the vulva is prone to infection. It may simply become dry and sore and a moisturising agent can give temporary relief, but as the season progresses the likelihood of uterine and vaginal infection increases, the culprit often being *Streptococcus* spp.

Prolonged oestrus can also result in *bone marrow disease*: aplastic anaemia with granulocytopaenia, thrombocytopaenia and hypocellular bone marrow. Clinical signs include depression, anorexia and pale mucous membranes. Associated conditions may result because of lowered immunity, and these may include alopecia and metritis. (However, bilaterally symmetrical alopecia of the tail and abdomen is quite common in oestrous females, and even in males in the breeding season, as is seasonal weight loss.) Treatment of bone marrow disease is lengthy and difficult (ref. Ryland, Lennox M., *A Clinical Guide to the Pet Ferret*) and not necessarily successful.

Termination of oestrus

Although some jills can remain unmated throughout the season without suffering any ill effects, we do advise that early steps should be taken to terminate oestrus one way or another in most jills. Spaying is the permanent solution. Mating is the most obvious course, with either an entire or a vasectomized hob, though an infertile mating will result in a pseudo-pregnancy lasting only some 42 days after which the jill will return to oestrus. Simulated mating, which includes prolonged rough and vigorous scruff-biting as much as vaginal stimulation, might be effective in inducing ovulation but is not something the ferret owner should be encouraged to attempt!

Hormonal treatment can be used to suppress the season and is now widely used by veterinary practices. Proligestone (Delvosteron, Mycofarm Ltd.) is now licensed for ferrets. The dose (0.5 ml subcut.) is best given in late March or early April. If given when oestrus has already started, the signs will subside within 5–7 days. Some jills seem habitually to return to oestrus 6–12 weeks later, when the same dose can be repeated. In the case of jills kept in artificial light, as mentioned above, it is likely that an early dose will be required and that it will need to be repeated later in the season.

The hormone injection is slightly irritant and ferrets tend to struggle to such an extent that sometimes the animal is released before the site has been properly massaged, with the result that a small patch of alopecia develops. It is important, therefore, that the owner should be asked to restrict the ferret until sufficient dispersal of the hormone has been effected.

If a jill has already been mated (accidentally) just before hormonal treatment, it must be borne in mind that there is a risk of foetuses having developed to a certain stage and then becoming mummified when hormone levels are artificially altered by the injection.

Pseudopregnancy

Pseudopregnancy is quite common and is the result of failed implantation, due possibly to photoperiodic factors, or male subfertility, or incidental vaginal stimulation. Its term is usually a day or two longer than the normal 42 days of a true pregnancy.

Pyometra (cystic hyperplasia of the endometrium)

Mated jills are susceptible to this condition a week or two after mating.

Cystic hyperplasia of the endometrium is a spontaneous condition (seen in bitches and queens as well as jills) in the post-oestrus phase, whether that phase is the result of a fertile or infertile mating: the lining of the womb can become hyperactive and produces large quantities of purulent secretion. The infection may clear up spontaneously but can persist in the uterine glands and erupt at a subsequent mating.

In some cases the resultant toxaemia can lead to peritonitis and sudden death, or to the rupturing of the uterus. The risk is much higher in the ferret than in other domestic species and urgent action must be taken. The only practical treatment is hysterectomy but even this might be unable to save the jill.

Pre-parturition

In the pre-parturition phase, eclamptogenic toxaemia has been known to result in the death of the dam and the unborn kits. It can be controlled by the addition of fresh raw liver in the pregnancy ration.

Parturition

Parturition is nearly always straightforward but may be prolonged by disturbance or excessive heat. There are several potential post-parturition problems, including endometritis (usually due to *Streptococcus* spp).

Mastitis, in which *E. coli* is present, is rapidly progressive with a potentially high mortality rate. Abscesses should be lanced and a topical antibiotic cream can be applied to the teats, or parenteral antibiotics can be administered.

Milk fever, with progressive posterior paresis, tremor, hyperaesthesia and convulsions, responds rapidly to calcium borogluconate injections.

Nursing sickness results from nutrition deficiencies. Symptoms include anorexia, weight loss, weakness, muscular incoordination, with death after a period of coma. It is usually observed in late June when the kits are weaned and it may be caused by insufficient dietary salt.

Haemolytic anaemia is reported from New Zealand, with loss of appetite and bodyweight, jaundice and red urine. Kits may die from starvation and the causes may include dietary oxidants (eg rancid fat). The source of polyunsaturated fats in the ration should be reduced, and stabilized vitamin E should be added. The ration could usefully include at least 5 per cent liver.

In wild mustelids, a major factor in controlling population numbers is reproductive failure, particularly stillbirths and failure to suckle. Pre-weaning kit deaths are sometimes quite high and arise from a variety of causes, most of them as the result of faulty management and nutrition. For example, wide diurnal temperature fluctuations may cause the jill to reject the kits.

Agalactia can result from dietary causes, excess heat or dehydration of the jill. Udder congestion, like mastitis, is a problem which is typical of many mammals. Failure of milk let-down can be treated by subcutaneous injection with oxytocin.

Other disorders in jills

Other reported disorders include non-malignant ovarian tumours in older jills, uterine leiomyomas being fairly common.

Vaginitis may be caused by the presence of foreign bodies in the vagina, such as hayseeds and barley awns from bedding, with secondary infection by a *Streptococcus* sp. This gives rise to a yellow mucropurulent vulval discharge, with in some cases secondary metritis and septicaemia. Treatment includes manual expulsion of the foreign body and use of parenteral long-acting penicillin.

BACTERIAL

Staphylococcus and Streptococcus spp

Abscesses are the most common reason for ferrets being brought into the surgery. The majority are around the mouth, jaw and neck (most frequently in the submaxillary area) and sometimes the groin and musk glands. Some ferrets can become quite ill with septicaemia.

The abscesses may arise as a result of injury from aggressive sexual neck-bites in the mating season, damage from bone splinters in the diet, dental infections, and general intrusion by foreign bodies (eg hayseeds and other bedding materials). In severe cases around the head, facial bones can be affected by osteomyelitis.

Staphylococcus aureus and *Streptococcus* spp are commonly involved. Surgical drainage (under anaesthetic if necessary) should be followed by appropriate antibiotic treatment and continued drainage.

Vulval and uterine infections are fairly common in jills, particularly in oestrus. Endometritis is often due to a streptococcal infection, and *Staphylococcus aureus* can cause mastitis. *Streptococcus zooepidemicus* can cause pneumonia and metritis in the ferret.

It should be noted that high doses of streptomycin are extremely toxic to ferrets and they should receive no more than 50 mg at 12-hour intervals.

Botulism due to Clostridium botulinum

Ferrets are particularly susceptible to type C botulism. Clinical signs include dysphagia, ataxia and paresis 12–96 hours after eating contaminated food. Limpness may be followed by paralysis of respiratory muscles and death. There is no successful treatment.

Salmonella

Salmonellosis is uncommon in ferrets, although it may cause pregnant females to abort.

Tuberculosis

Although tuberculosis is now rare in this country, ferrets are susceptible to avian, bovine and human mycobacteria and the disease might be introduced by contact with infected bird droppings or the consumption of infected offal or tuberculosis-infected milk. Clinical signs tend to be masked until the disease is well advanced, when there may be rapid emaciation with paralysis of the pelvic adductor muscles (and later of all four limbs), enteritis and swollen mesenteric lymph glands. The disease is likely to be fatal.

Other bacterial infections

There have been reported cases of *E. coli* being involved in enteritis and, in North America but very rarely in the UK, of *Campylobacter fetus* (subsp. *jejuni*) in proliferative colitis. A 'warm weather' enteritis can lead to acute cases with bloody diarrhoea, anorexia and death within 3–4 days. Chronic enteritis, with intermittent diarrhoea and normal appetite but failure to digest, with subsequent emaciation and death within a month if untreated, may respond in the early stages to neomycin (10–20 mg/kg) and kaolin.

Ferrets can be affected subclinically by brucellosis, tularaemia and listeria monocytogenes. Anthrax has been recorded in ferrets. The signs are haemorrhaging from the mouth and rectum and sudden death. The ferrets had been fed meat from a beef animal which died suddenly. An appropriate antibiotic injection given to exposed ferrets will stop the infection developing.

VIRAL

Because of their susceptibility, ferrets have been used extensively in laboratory investigations into canine distemper and human influenza. They are highly susceptible to distemper, which proves fatal in most cases. Common colds and influenza are contagious between ferrets and humans: infected owners should keep away from their animals.

Canine distemper

The distemper source can be direct contact with dogs or dog urine, or indirect contact through humans handling unvaccinated dogs. Ferrets taken to country shows run particular risks. Routine vaccination against canine distemper is recommended (see Vaccination, p. 159).

Incubation may be as much as 10 days after exposure. Initial signs 7–10 days after exposure include loss of appetite: little or nothing will be eaten thereafter. There is watery discharge from the eyes, becoming purulent so that the lids adhere, and there is also a mucropurulent nasal discharge. By the tenth or twelfth day there are usually skin pustules under the chin and in the inguinal area; foot pads may swell and become hyperkeratotic (note that this is similar to footrot). The anus is likely to protrude. Continuing deterioration leads to death at 12–14 days from ferret-adapted strains or at 21–24 days from canine strains.

Animals that survive the catarrhal phase may die in a neurotropic episode: hyperexcitability, excess salivation, muscular tremor, convulsions and coma – similar to the signs of chorea in dogs.

Diagnosis can be confirmed by virus isolation or by pathological examination for characteristic inclusion bodies in urinary bladder and trachea.

There is no specific treatment for distemper in ferrets, although mild cases may recover with nursing. All cages and equipment must be thoroughly disinfected and sterilized.

Influenza

Within 48 hours of exposure, the ferret becomes quiet and listless. Its rectal temperature rises sharply to 40–41°C. The nose is moist and food is refused. Pyrexia lasts for a day, then returns on the third day. There may be sneezing attacks and a purulent nasal discharge. Antihistamines may relieve congestion. The animal becomes more lively as soon as the second peak has subsided, and it recovers quickly and on the whole uneventfully. Immunity after recovery is effective for at least 5 weeks against homologous strains of influenza.

Occasionally more severe cases develop with anorexia and pneumonia leading to death within about two months, but there may be no immunological relationship between the virus of this disease and human influenza.

Infection by human influenza virus induces mild upper respiratory symptoms in mature, healthy ferrets but in very young kits or aged and debilitated mature animals the infection can prove fatal. It is wise to give antibiotic treatment to control secondary infection while symptoms persist.

Aleutian disease

Named from the Aleutian strain of mink in the USA (in which it was first discovered in 1956), this disease is caused by a slow parvovirus. It has been recorded in ferrets in North America and New Zealand, and was first recognized in UK ferrets in 1990. There is circumstantial evidence of a link with mink: in several cases in southern England, infected colonies have included stray ferrets found in areas where feral mink were present. The disease is known to be present in ranched mink in Britain.

At least four strains of the virus affect mink in the USA and it is probable that there is also a ferret strain. Ferrets are closely related to mink and have been deliberately interbred with them to increase the number of litters on mink ranches. It is therefore quite possible that feral mink would associate with stray ferrets, and it is probable that the virus is endemic in feral mink in the UK.

Aleutian is an immune-mediated disease, its symptoms being due to excessive stimulation of the immune reaction to the virus. Symptoms vary: they can include weight loss and progressive wasting, thirst, black tarry faeces, sometimes bleeding from the gums, and in several cases posterior ataxia and paresis in domestic ferrets presented as 'going off their legs'. Incidence in the UK is low at present. There is no treatment and the only sensible course is regular screening and isolation. It is important that premises are thoroughly disinfected, as the virus remains very resistant outside the body.

Members of the Wessex Ferret Club have participated in a screening programme and survey conducted by Welchman, Oxenham and Done (*Vet.Rec.* (1993) 132, 479–484). Animals that test positive are not necessarily shedding the virus: the test simply shows that the ferret has been exposed to the virus at some time and has subsequently developed antibodies. In some which have tested serologically positive, the virus persists, whereas in others it gradually wanes. Full details of testing and survey results are available from Oxenham at Beech House Veterinary Centre, Bitterne, Southampton.

Posterior paralysis should alert the veterinarian to the possibility of Aleutian disease but there are several other potential causes. Examples have been cited of viral encephalomyelitis (though the virus has not been identified), hypocalcaemia in nursing jills, spinal dysplasia, bone marrow disease and dietary imbalance as well as vertebral trauma. Ferreters tend to use the term 'staggers' for a symptom whose several possible causes are not always easy to distinguish clinically.

Leukaemia

Leukaemia is very rare in the UK. In theory it may occur in young ferrets between 9 and 18 months of age, or occasionally in older animals. In the younger group there is very little warning and death is sudden. In older animals the virus acts slowly and there may be signs of lymphoblast-type tumours behind the jaw, in the groin or along the abdomen. The condition seems to be more common in males than in females.

PARASITES AND FUNGI

Ferrets suffer from many of the same parasites as dogs and cats and treatment is for the most part similar. IVOMEC (MSD Agvet) is an effective parasiticidal preparation for use in ferrets but it appears to be teratogenic and can cause congenital abnormalities in the foetus: it should not be used during pregnancy.

Skin allergies are not often seen in the ferret. Ticks and fleas, on the other hand, are very common.

Sarcoptes scabiei

This may be involved in footrot, a condition in which the feet become swollen, painful and scabby (though swollen feet may also be indicative of distemper). In extreme cases the claws drop out. The initial cause is damp and dirty quarters.

Treatment is by Ivomec injection. Cages must be thoroughly disinfected with a hot, strong solution of washing soda, and all bedding must be burned.

Sarcoptic mange over other parts of the body produces general alopecia, skin lesions and intense pruritis. Carbaryl (0.5 per cent) shampoos may be effective.

Otodectes cynotis

Infection with this ear mite is very common in the ferret but does not seem to cause trouble in the majority of cases. Occasionally, secondary infection and middle-ear disease might be complications.

The mite causes inflammation and irritation of the ears, leading to scratching and head shaking, with granular brown debris in the external auditory canal. The debris may contain fungi such as *Absidia corymbifera*. In middle-ear disease the animal's head will be tilted to one side or turned towards one flank; it may lose its balance and turn circles, and prostration and death can follow: the ear drum can be ruptured and the middle ear infected, followed by invasion of the inner ear and cranium, meninges and brain.

Treatment is by Ivomec injection or drops.

Microsporum canis

Ringworm has been reported, possibly transmitted by cats – the ferret is probably an accidental rather than natural host. Signs: hair loss with dry scaly patches which gradually enlarge. Griseofulvin (25 mg/kg) can be given orally, but the clinical signs often regress spontaneously. Regrowth of hair will probably not recommence for two or three weeks, and in the albino it may well be of a darker shade at first.

Griseofulvin has also been used successfully to treat the early stages of an ulcerative dermatitis of unknown cause in kits as young as one week old. *Candida albicans* may be present. Early lesions, similar to ringworm, are

small, discrete and circular; they progress to large, moist lesions with loss of
fur and discoloration of the skin. The lesions tend to be on the back, belly,
inner thighs and tail.

Ctenocephalides spp (Fleas)
Flea infestations are very common, particularly on working ferrets during
the summer months. Infestations can rapidly build up and if there are several
hundred feeding on a ferret, a severe and fatal anaemia can develop. There
are two new and very effective products.
(a) Frontline (Rhône-Merieux) pump action spray.
(b) Droplix (Virbac) 0.10 ml liquid to the skin over the neck/shoulder area.
Both these preparations are applied at intervals of 1–2 months depending on
the severity of the infestation. Never use more than one insecticide at the
same time.

Ixodes spp (Ticks)
Ticks are often found on ferrets, but even when present in considerable
numbers, they do not appear to unduly harm the animal. Ticks overwinter
in the depths and warmth of rabbit burrows and working ferrets are those
that are mainly at risk. Ticks can be removed physically with appropriate
tweezers after being soaked with alcohol.

Endoparasites
Ferrets do not appear to be the natural hosts of any gastrointestinal helminths
but there may be 'accidental' infections with *Toxocara* spp. Regular worming
is probably unnecessary but, if the need arises, useful treatments include
fenbendazole (Panacur Wormer 22% granules; Hoechst; 0.5g/kg for a single
dose) or mebendazole (50 mg/kg b.i.d. for 2 days).
   Ferrets may be susceptible to coccidiosis, cryptococcosis, toxoplasmosis
and actinomycosis.

NEOPLASMS
Various spontaneous tumours have been observed in ferrets, as in other
species seen in the surgery, but incidence in the UK is low. It is interesting
to note that the incidence of certain tumours is very high in the USA as
compared with UK. The main sources of ferrets in the USA are enormous
breeding units, some producing 2000 kits a week. It is their practice to neuter
the kits at 5–6 weeks of age and sell them 2 weeks later. The question
therefore arises as to whether this *modus operandi* is causing the high incidence
or adrenal adenoma, insulinoma and lymphosarcoma. Adrenal adenomas
arise in either of the two very important endocrine (hormone) glands near

each kidney. The mainly benign tumous produce high levels of sex hormones, which in the neutered female initiate oestrus symptoms and alopecia, and in the neutered male, prostate enlargement and urinary difficulties.

Insulominas occur in the pancreas, and produce abnormally high levels of insulin, which depresses the blood sugar to dangerous levels.

Veterinary surgeons are well aware of the endocrine tumours, but, to date, there is no published record of them occurring in the UK.

Lymphosarcoma do, of course, occur in the UK and arise in many different organs and sites, but, again, the incidence is very low.

The cause of these serious problems in the USA is probably due to factors such as genetic predisposition, the presence of an oncogenic (cancer causing) virus, extreme early neutering and some veterinarians have suggested a dietary factor as well.

In the UK, primary tumours have been recorded in most sites of the body, with the notable exception of the central nervous system, osteosarcomas and carcinomas of the lung. These either don't occur or are exceptionally rare. Another unusual feature is that different, non-metastatic tumours have been found in the one individual.

Many tumours, particularly of the reproductive tract, skin and superficial glands, can be treated satisfactorily by surgery. However, the more malignant internal tumours would need chemotherapy, which is usually deemed too expensive for ferrets.

CALCULI
There have been reported cases of cystic and renal calculi. Urolithiasis can be fatal and is probably most common in castrated males, particularly on dry diets. Treatment is as for feline urolithiasis and cystitis.

POISONING
Zinc poisoning has been a problem with laboratory ferrets, and the use of galvanized feeding or water utensils or cage-wire should be discouraged. Clinical signs include anaemia and posterior weakness, and death seems to be inevitable. *Nitrates* in fishmeal (herring preservative) when heated to form feed pellets may produce carcinogenic tumours in ferrets.
Snake-bites are rare in this country, although polecats are known to kill snakes and are said to be immune to adder venom! It may be that lethal doses are not injected.

NUTRITIONAL, METABOLIC AND MISCELLANEOUS PROBLEMS
Incorrect nutrition is one of the major causes of unusual 'symptoms', such

as enteritis and skeletal problems, or even posterior paralysis. Many owners find that day-old chicks are a convenient source of food for ferrets but the chicks retain a high proportion of egg yolk. If they are given to the exclusion of all other foods this can lead to nutritional deficiencies, such as thiamin (the signs of which include lethargy, lack of appetite, hindquarter weakness and terminal convulsions).

Rickets (*Osteodystrophia fibrosa*) is in fact hyperphosphorosis associated with dietary imbalance in a rapidly growing kit between the ages of about 6–12 weeks. The problem usually affects the whole litter to a greater or lesser extent, and in some litters there can be quite a high mortality rate. Frequently the presenting sign is sudden death in kits, post-weaning. The surviving kits in the litter have rubbery, deformed leg bones which are easily broken; they are unable to support their own weight, are reluctant to move and have difficulty in walking normally. They tend to assume a posture resembling a breaststroke swimmer, with the back legs trailing.

The recommendation for prevention in kits is to ensure adequate calcium intake and a good Ca:P ratio by including 5–10 per cent sterilized bone-meal in the diet or by supplementing all-meat diets with 2 per cent bone flour or 2 per cent dicalcium phosphate. The post-weaning diet is crucial. There are now commercial foods specifically for pet ferrets but tinned or dried kitten foods (not adult cat foods, the nutritional content of which is too variable) seem to be ideal for young ferrets.

Haemolytic anaemia may result from rations rich in polyunsaturated fats (PUFA), especially in lactating jills. It can be controlled by dietary regulation and possibly treated by subcutaneous applications of 0.1 mg sodium selenite and 1 mg alphatocopherol acetate.

Yellow fat disease (nutritional steatitis) is caused by vitamin E deficiency or feeding diets containing high levels of PUFA (eg oily fish, horse meat or slink meat). Growing kits are more susceptible than adults and can contract the disease prior to weaning. Kits may die suddenly. Other symptoms are depression, reluctance to move, pain in the lower abdomen, and firm sub-cutaneous swellings in inguinal and flank regions. There may also be loss of appetite, respiratory distress, hind-leg weakness, diarrhoea with black faeces, and evidence of pain when the animal is handled. Treatment, where is it not too late, is by giving 10–20 mg Vitamin E per day and reducing PUFA levels in the diet.

Fatty liver/agalactia syndrome (eclamptogenic toxaemia) may be prevalent among nursing jills. Clinical signs: acute onset of agalactia, depression and lethargy; kits dying of starvation. Recovery follows removal of the litter to a foster mother. Diets rich in PUFA (eg those high in chicken offal) should be supplemented with antioxidant and Vitamin E.

Alopecia may be a result of excessive amounts of raw egg in the diet, causing a biotin deficiency which may be corrected by feeding raw liver during pregnancy. There are many other causes of alopecia, including tumours of the adrenals and ovaries, ectoparasites, dietary and unknown.

Gastric Ulceration The signs of this will be dysphagia, haematemesis, weight loss and depression. The cause has been identified as Helicobacter musteli and if caught early, it should respond to treatment with metronidazole.

Gastrointestinal foreign bodies such as pieces of rubber, and also hairballs, are sometimes the cause of a visit to the surgery, often (but not always) with vomiting as a presenting sign. Other symptoms include anorexia and diarrhoea. Identification of the problem is by abdominal palpation or radiography and the object can often be removed surgically.

Diabetes mellitus has been recorded in a few ferrets and successfully treated.

Heatstroke is a common problem. Ferrets are unable to lose heat readily and are quickly overcome in hot weather. Emergency treatment entails rapid cooling by all possible means. As the lungs offer the greatest area of exposure, efforts should be made to introduce cold air as well as drenching the animal in cold water.

Congestive heart failure occurs in ferrets. It is usually in animals over 6–7 years of age and the signs are malaise, poor appetite, wasting of muscles, ascites and pleural fluid with dyspnoea. Supportive treatment with diuretics can be given, but the prognosis is poor.

Chronic renal failure is seen mainly in old ferrets. The signs are malaise, poor appetite, weight loss, increased thirst, and poor teeth. Diagnosis can be confirmed by an appropriate blood profile.

Ferret Facts

ADULT WEIGHT	1–5½ lbs (500 g–2.5 kg). Very wide range, and varies considerably according to time of year (up to 40 per cent).
ADULT DIMENSIONS	17–24 ins (44–60 cm) including tail. Male can be twice as large as female.
AVERAGE LIFESPAN	5–6 years in laboratory. Up to 10 years pets (older have been known).
CHROMOSOME COUNT	40.
RESPIRATORY RATE	30–40 per minute.
HEART RATE	220–250 beats per minute.
RECTAL TEMP.	Average 38.8C (101.8F). Range 37.8–40C (100–104F).

TEETH	Incisors 3/3, Canines 1/1, Premolars 3/3, Molars 1/2. Supernumerary incisors common.
TOES	5 on each foot.
NIPPLES	8 (male and female).
VERTEBRAE	C7, T14, L6, S3, COL14-18. 14 pairs of ribs.
OTHER ANATOMY	No caecum, appendix, male prostate gland. Sweat glands not well developed.
ENVIRONMENT	Optimum 15-20C (60-70F max.). Heat prostration likely at 32C (90F).
SEXING	Ano-genital distance of male at least twice that of female.
PUBERTY	240-250 days.
SEXUAL MATURITY	9-12 months, or the spring following birth.
AGE TO BREED	M 365 days, F 275 days. 1st mating possible at 6 months.
BREEDING SEASON	Photoperiodically triggered - possibly 16 hours daylight, but see HAMMOND (Bibl.). Main breeding season March-August in Britain (male testes begin to descend Dec./Jan. and regress by July, female in oestrus any time from March to October).
SEASON SIGNS	Female: swollen vulva. Male: swollen testes.
DURATION OF OESTRUS	Continuous until mated or until end of season and very prolonged if unmated. Ovulation induced by male stimulus (behaviour and coitus).
DURATION OF MATING	10 minutes to several hours - probably 1 hour on average.
OVULATION	30 hours after mating.
REDUCTION OF VULVA	7-10 days, complete within 2-3 weeks of mating.
PALPATION	10 days after vulva reduced.
GESTATION	Average 42 days. (Range 38-44 days; at 45 days kits die.)
LITTERS PER YEAR	Two possible (up to 5 under controlled photoperiod).
NESTING	Starts building 10-12 days before birth.
OTHER BIRTH SIGNS	Mammary glands.
POST-NATAL OESTRUS	1-2 weeks after weaning.
LITTER SIZE	2-17 (average 8, norm. 6-9) - more in first litter of season than in second.
BIRTHWEIGHT	$\frac{1}{2}$ oz (5-15 g).
DECIDUOUS TEETH	Begin to erupt at 10-14 days.
CANINES	47-52 days.
EYES/EARS OPEN	21-37 days.
FUR	Almost naked at birth, some by 9 days, good woolly coat by 4-5 weeks.
OUT OF NEST	First ventures usually 3-4 weeks.
WEANING AGE	6-8 weeks.
WEANING WEIGHT	$10\frac{1}{2}$-$17\frac{1}{2}$ oz (300-500 g).
ATTAIN ADULT WEIGHT	4 months.
1st POSSIBLE MATING	6 months.
1st NORMAL MATING	12 months.

Nutrition Tables

TABLE A: NUTRITION GUIDE

(DRY BASIS)

	FITCH	MINK
Protein	40% minimum	25-32%
Fat	15-40%	9%
Ash (from bone)	5-15%	
Non-fat energy and fibre	12-25%	
Calcium	1.0-1.2%	0.3%
Phosphorus	1.0%	0.3%
Salt	0.5-1.0%	0.5%
Iron		114 mg/kg
Vitamin A		10,000 IU
Vitamin E	*250 mg/kg min.	25 IU
SOURCES	*Surveillance* Vol. 11, No. 2, New Zealand Ministry of Agriculture and Fisheries, 1984.	*Nutrient Requirements of Mink and Foxes* Vol. 7, National Academy of Sciences, Washington DC, 1968.
NOTES	Recommended ranges for dry ration, assuming energy content is about 5,000 kcal/kg. Levels given are sometimes in excess of required levels for ordinary rations – eg vitamin E.	Based on diet with metabolizable energy concentration of 4.25 kcal/g of DM.

*NRC recommend only 25 mg/kg (DMB) vitamin E for those mink which are fed rations not prone to rancidity. In rations known to cause Yellow Fat Disease in mink, the addition of 300 mg/kg (DMB) prevents the disease. Ryland & Gorham (*Journal of the American Veterinary Medical Association*, 173: 1154; 1978) recommend 10 mg per day per ferret; this is approximately equivalent to 250 mg/kg (DMB). Vitamin E is relatively non-toxic.

TABLE B: PROXIMATE ANALYSIS OF FEEDSTUFFS

Feedstuff	Dry Matter %	Protein % (WMB)	Fat % (WMB)	Ash % (WMB)
Boned mutton	25	18	14	3.4
Slink meat	32	15	13	3.4
Chicken (layers)	47	22	18	4.0
Day-old chicks	24	17	6	1.8
Chicken heads/necks etc	45	13	25	4.0
Boned beef	28	22	4	0.3
Beef liver	29	20	4	1.0
Fish heads and racks	20	14	2	4.8
Goat carcase	25	16	6	3.4
Horse meat	26	20	4	1.0
Bones	65	20	15	29.0
Cooked eggs	33	13	11	3.0

(*Source: Surveillance* Vol. 11, No. 2, 1984)

TABLE C: ANALYSIS OF FERRET MILK

Element	Ferret %	Human %	Sheep %	Goat %	Buffalo %	Cow (Fr'sn) %
Total solids	23.5					
Fat	8.0	3.7	7.5	4.5	7.4	3.5
Proteins	6.0	2.0	5.6	3.3	3.8	3.2
Lactose	3.8					
Ash	0.8					

Adapted from: Lactation, a Comprehensive Treaty (R. Jenness's chapter on 'Composition of Milk') and *Food Production* (Open University)

Glossary

ALBINO	Animal with pink eyes. The coat may be white, cream, or a deeper yellowy-orange.
BITCH	Term for a female ferret – *see also* DOE and JILL.
BLEEPER	Electronic device for locating lost ferret – *see also* FERRET FINDER.
BOLTING	Using a ferret to persuade a rabbit or rat to leave a safe place in a hurry. Many other animals will bolt from an underground run if a ferret is behind them.
BUCK	Term for a male ferret (*see also* DOG and HOB) or a male rabbit.
BURROW or BURY	Refuge of linked underground passages and chambers used by rabbits, with various entrances and bolt-holes.
CHINNING	Method of killing a rabbit quickly and cleanly by pushing its head sharply up and back with your palm under its chin.
CHOPPING	Method of killing a rabbit by striking sharply at the base of its skull with the side of your hand, karate style. Difficult to kill with one blow (may only stun) and will bruise the meat.
DEAD END	Bury tunnel leading nowhere, often an abandoned excavation or a chamber scraped out as a nest at the end of a tunnel.
DOE	Term for female ferret (*see also* BITCH and JILL) or female rabbit.
DOG	Term for male ferret – *see also* BUCK and HOB.
DRESSING OUT	Removing a dead rabbit's gut. *See also* PAUNCHING. (Sometimes called 'evisceration'!)
FERAL	Escaped domesticated animal living in the wild.
FERRET	Domesticated polecat. Some people use the term only for an ALBINO, but ferrets come in many different colours, shapes and sizes. Sometimes labelled *Mustela putorius furo*, the *furo* tag differentiating it from the wild polecat.
FERRETING	Working with a ferret to bolt rabbits or rats.
FERRET FINDER	*See* BLEEPER.
FLECK	Rabbit fluff.
FITCH	Ferret fur.
FITCHET	*See* HYBRID.
GRAFT	Narrow ditching spade for digging out a ferret or a rabbit. Has a curved blade.
GREYHOUND	Fast-moving, long, lean ferret.
HEAT	Jills 'on heat' are in a condition to be mated and will respond to a hob's advances.
HOB	Specifically, a male ferret. Sometimes called DOG or BUCK.
HOBBLE	Castrated hob.
HYBRID	First cross between wild polecat and ferret. Also called FITCHET.
JILL	Specifically, a female ferret. Sometimes called BITCH or DOE.

KILLING DOWN	Killing a rabbit underground.
KIT	Young ferret, part of a LITTER.
LINER	Large, bullying hob kept separately from other ferrets and sent down to chase a lying-up ferret off its kill. The liner's position in a bury can be traced by the line attached to its collar. It should stay on the kill until you dig it out.
LITTER	Family of kits of the same age and from the same mother.
LURCHER	*See* GREYHOUND.
LYING UP	Staying underground after killing down, to eat the kill and have a postprandial snooze.
MASK	Facial markings, particularly in a polecat or poley.
MITTS	Feet, especially if of a different colouring to the main body coat.
MUSK	Scent produced by anal glands.
NECK-BREAKING	Method of killing a rabbit quickly, cleanly and humanely by stretching its neck.
OESTRUS	State in which a jill is ready for mating, or on heat. The adjective is 'oestrous'. If an oestrous jill is not mated she remains on heat for up to six months in a condition known as 'prolonged oestrus'.
OVULATION	The release of ripe eggs so that they can be fertilized by sperm. Ferret ovulation is induced naturally by the physical acts of courtship and mating. When ovulation has been induced, the female is no longer in oestrus.
PAUNCHING	Removing a dead rabbit's guts.
PHOTOPERIODISM	Dependence on length of daylight to trigger certain reactions. Ferrets are photoperiodic breeders: they are triggered into breeding condition by specific conditions of day-length.
POLECAT	Wild species from which ferrets were first domesticated several thousand years ago.
POLECAT-FERRET or POLEY	Ferret with markings similar to a polecat's but not necessarily a first cross between a wild polecat and a ferret (*see* HYBRID).
POPHOLE	Easily overlooked emergency exit from a bury. Often on flatter ground a little way from other holes, going down almost vertically rather than angled into a slope. Usually of small diameter and often covered with leaves or grass.
PURSE NET	Net with drawstring running through rings. Forms an instant pouch or purse around a bolting rabbit as it leaves the hole.
SANDY	Ferrets of all colours between pure ALBINO and POLECAT. White sandies have dark eyes rather than the pink of the true albino.
SIAMESE	Pale ferret with dark brown legs.
SILVER	Ferret with white undercoat and 'silver' guard hairs mixed in with normal guard hairs.
SILVER MITT	Ferret with white feet.

SWEATS	Heatstroke.
THUMBING	Using a thumb to express a dead rabbit's urine before paunching, to avoid tainting the meat.
WARREN	Large and complex bury system. The original warrens were man-made and carefully enclosed so that rabbits could be harvested for meat and fur. Full-time warreners were responsible for them.

Useful Addresses

Organizations

NATIONAL FERRET WELFARE SOCIETY
For information please send a large SAE to
N.F.W.S.
6 St. Edmond Road
Bedford MK40 2NQ
Tel: 01234–272769

PEOPLE'S DISPENSARY FOR SICK ANIMALS
Whitechapel Way
Priorslee
Telford Shropshire TF2 9PQ

ROYAL SOCIETY FOR PREVENTION OF CRUELTY
TO ANIMALS
The Manor House
Causeway
Horsham West Sussex

UNIVERSITIES FEDERATION FOR ANIMAL
WELFARE
8 Hamilton Close
South Mimms
Potters Bar Middlesex

Pharmaceutical and Other Companies supplying products which have been used for ferrets:

BEECHAM ANIMAL HEALTH
Beecham House
Brentford Middlesex TW9 8BD

CEVA LTD
PO Box 209
3 Rhodes Way
Watford Herts WD2 4QE

CROWN CHEMICAL CO LTD
Lamberhurst Kent TN3 8DJ

CYANAMID OF GREAT BRITAIN LTD
Animal Health Division
154 Fareham Road
Gosport Hants PO13 0AS

GLAXOVET LTD
Harefield
Uxbridge Middlesex UB9 6LS

HOECHST UK LTD
Walton Manor
Walton
Milton Keynes Bucks MK7 7AJ

MANSI LABORATORIES LTD
Herons Way
Wey Road
Weybridge Surrey KT13 8HS

MYCOFARM UK LTD
Science Park
Milton Road
Cambridge CB4 4FP
Tel: 01223 423971
Fax: 01233 420504

PARKE-DAVIS VETERINARY
Usk Road
Pontypool Gwent NP4 0YH

TASMAN VACCINE LABORATORY (UK) LTD
Eastern Way
Bury St. Edmunds Suffolk IP32 7AL

UPJOHN LTD
Fleming Way
Crawley West Sussex RH10 2NJ

VETERINARY DRUG CO PLC
129-135 Lawrence Street
York YO1 3EG

THE WELLCOME FOUNDATION LTD
Crewe Hall
Crewe Cheshire CW1 1UB

ASHE LABORATORIES LTD (SHIRLEY'S)
Leatherhead Surrey

CATAC PRODUCTS LTD
Catac House
1 Newnham Street
Bedford

Bibliography

BOOKS AND BOOKLETS

BAILEY, Adrian (Ed.): *Mrs Bridges' Upstairs Downstairs Cookery Book* (Sphere Books, 1975)

BEDSON, G.: *The Notorious Poacher* (Saiga, 1981)

BENYON, P.H., and COOPER, J.E.: *Manual of Exotic Pets* (BSAVA, 3rd edition, 1991)

BUCKLAND, Martin D., HALL, Lynda, MOWLEM, Alan, WHATLEY, Beryl: *A Guide to Laboratory Animal Technology* (Wm. Heinemann Medical Books Ltd, 1981)

CARTHY, J.D.: *The Study of Behaviour* (Edward Arnold, rev. 1979)

CLARK, Michael: *Mammal Watching* (Severn House Naturalists Library, 1981)

CRAIG, Elizabeth: *Economical Cookery* (Collins, 1948)

DRABBLE, Philip: *Pleasing Pets* (Wm. Luscombe, 1975)

—— *A Weasel in my Meatsafe* (Michael Joseph, 1977)

ENCYCLOPAEDIA BRITANNICA, 1926 edition

EVANS, J.M. (Ed.): *The Henston Veterinary Vade Mecum* (Henston Ltd, 1984)

Editor of *Exchange & Mart: Ferrets & Ferreting - A Practical Guide on their Breeding, Managing, Training and Working*

Farmers Weekly: Farmhouse Fare (Hulton Press, 1950)

FERMOR, M.G.P.: *Home Pets, Furred & Feathered* (C. Arthur Pearson Ltd, 1902)

The GAME CONSERVANCY: *Rabbit Control* (MAFF, 1980)

GILBERTSON and PAGE: *Poachers versus Keepers* (reprinted by Tideline Books, 1983; first printed by Gilbertson & Page Ltd, Hertford, 1894)

HARRISON MATTHEWS, L.: *British Mammals* (Collins New Naturalist series, 2nd edition, 1968)

JEFFERIES, Richard: *The Amateur Poacher* (Thos. Nelson & Sons)

KANABLE, Ann: *Raising Rabbits* (Rodale Press, 1977)

KIRK, Robert W.: *First Aid for Pets* (Pelham, 1979)

LARSON, Bruce L., SMITH, Vearl R. (Eds.): *Lactation, a Comprehensive Treatise* (Academic Press, 1969)

LAWRENCE, M.J., BROWN, R.W.: *Mammals of Britain - Their Tracks, Trails and Signs* (Blandford Press, 1973)

LEVER, Christopher: *The Naturalized Animals of the British Isles* (Hutchinson, 1977)

LEWINGTON, J.H.: *Ferrets: A Compendium* (The T.G. Hungerford Vade Mecum series for domestic animals, Series C Number 10; University of Sydney Post Graduate Foundation in Veterinary Science, Australia, 1988)

LOCKLEY, R.M.: *The Private Life of the Rabbit* (Deutsch, 1965)

MACDONALD, David (Ed.): *The Encyclopaedia of Mammals* (Geo. Allen & Unwin, 1984)

MARCHINGTON, J.: *Pugs and Drummers - Ferrets and Rabbits in Britain* (Faber & Faber, 1978)

MASON, I.L. (Ed.): *Evolution of Domesticated Animals* (chapter on ferrets by Clifford Owen) (Longman Group Ltd, 1984)

McFARLAND, David (Ed.): *The Oxford Companion to Animal Behaviour* (Oxford University Press, 1981)

McKAY, J.: *Ferrets and Ferreting Handbook* (Crowood Press, 1989)

MEDAWAR, P.B. & J.S.: *Aristotle to Zoos – A Philosophical Dictionary of Biology* (Weidenfeld & Nicholson, 1984)

NIALL, Ian: *The New Poacher's Handbook* (Wm. Heinemann, 1960)

ORBIS: *World of Wildlife – The North: Animals of Moorland & Forest* (Orbis, 1971–4)

PARKER, Eric (Ed.): *Shooting by Moor, Field and Shore* (Lonsdale Library – Seeley, Service & Co, 1934)

PDSA: *Keeping a Ferret* (leaflet)

PLUMMER, D.B.: *Modern Ferreting* (The Boydell Press, Ipswich, 1977)

POOLE, Trevor B.: *Polecats* (Forest Record 76, Forestry Commission, 1970)

ROBERTS, Mervin F.: *All About Ferrets* (TFH Publications Inc, 1977)

RSPCA: *The Ferret* (leaflet)

SAMUEL, E., and IVESTER LLOYD, J.: *Rabbiting & Ferreting* (British Field Sports Society booklet, 8th ed., 1982)

SHORT, D.J. and WOODNOTT, D.P.: 1969 I.A.T. *Manual of Laboratory Animal Practice and Techniques* (2nd ed., Crosby Lockwood, 1969)

SMITH, Guy N.: *Ferreting and Trapping for Amateur Gamekeepers* (Spur Publications, 1978)

SPAULDING, C.E.: *A Veterinary Guide for Animal Owners* (Rodale Press Inc, Emmary PA, 1976)

STEPHENS, Wilson (Ed.): *The Field Bedside Book* (Collins, 1967)

STODDART, Michael D.: *Mammalian Odours and Pheromones* (Edward Arnold, 1976)

TAYLOR, Fred. J.: *One for the Pot – Game and Fish Cookbook* (Adam & Charles Black, 1979)

—— *Shooting Times Guide to Ferreting* (Percival Marshall, 1979)

TITTENSOR, M.M. and LLOYD, H.G.: *Rabbits* (Forestry Commission, FC Forest Record 125, 1983)

TURNBULL, Colin: *The Mountain People* (Jonathan Cape, 1974)

UFAW: *5th UFAW Handbook on the Care & Management of Laboratory Animals* (Universities Federation for Animal Welfare – Chapter 9: The Ferret, by J.H. Hammond Jr)

—— *Self-awareness in Domestic Animals*

—— *The Welfare and Management of Wild Animals in Captivity*

—— *The Humane Control of Animals Living in the Wild*

VEYSEY-FITZGERALD, Brian: *It's My Delight* (1947 – reprinted by Tideline Books, 1978)

WELLSTEAD, Graham: *The Ferret and Ferreting Guide* (David & Charles, 1981)

WEST, Anthony: *The Ferret Fancier* (Simon & Schuster, NY, 1963)

WHITAKER, Peter: *Ferrets & Ferreting* (Pugs & Drummers, 1978)

WINSTED, Wendy: *Ferrets* (TFH Publications, NJ, 1981)

YOST, Sid, et al: *What's a Ferret?* (private publication, 1977)

REFERENCES

BERNARD, Susan L., LEATHERS, Charles W., BROBST, Duane F., GORHAM, John R.: 'Estrogen-induced bone marrow depression in ferrets' (*Am. J. Vet. Res*, Vol. 44, No. 4, April 1983, pp. 657ff)

BRISTOW-NOBLE, J.C.: 'A tame polecat' (*The Field* 152: 74, 1928)

BUCKWELL, Tony: 'Persistent oestrus' (letter to *The Veterinary Record*, July 1981)

DASH, J.D. and ALLEN, P.S.C.: 'Spaying ferrets' (letter to *The Veterinary Record*, April 1979)

FLECKNELL, Paul: 'Restraint, anaesthesia and treatment of children's pets' (*In Practice*, May 1983)

HAMMOND, J.: 'Notes on Ovulation and Fertilisation in the Ferret' (Reprint from *Journal of Experimental Biology*, Vol. XI, No. 3, pp. 307-25, July 1934)

HAMMOND, J. Jr: 'The Ferret: Some observations on Photoperiod and Gonadal Activity and their role in seasonal Pelt and Bodyweight changes; the synergistic effect of oestrogen and progesterone on weight gain; and a comparative study of the Corpus Luteum of the Ferret and the rabbit' (dist. by W. Heffer & Sons Ltd, Cambridge, 1974)

HART, D.S.: 'Photoperiodicity in the Female Ferret' (*Journal of Experimental Biology*, Vol. 28, No. 1, pp. 1-10, March 1951)

HOWELL, J.M.: 'Disappearance of polecats' (*The Field* 162, 1933)

JOHNSTONE, Ian: 'Hawking with ferrets' (*The Falconer*, 1979)

JONES, John L.: 'Polecat or ferret?' (*Country Life*, June 1954)

KNIGHT, John A.: 'Veterinary and pathological aspects of keeping wild canids and mustelids' (Proceedings of Symposium 5 of The Association of British Wild Animal Keepers)

KOCIBA, Gary J. and CAPUTO, Cheryl A.: 'Aplastic Anemia associated with Estrus in Pet Ferrets' (*JAVMA*, Vol. 178, No. 12, June 15, 1981, pp. 1293 ff)

LEWINGTON, J.H.: 'Handling ferrets' (letter to *The Veterinary Record*, June 25, 1983)

LIBERSON, A.J. et al: 'Mastitis caused by hemolytic *Escherichia coli* in the ferret' (*JAVMA*, Vol. 183, No. 11, 1 December 1983)

MACMANUS, D.: 'Taming a ferret' (*The Field* 168, 1936)

OXENHAM, M.: 'Oestrus control in the ferret' (letter to *Veterinary Practice*, October 5, 1992)

PITT, F.: 'Where the foumart holds its own' (*The Field* 156, 1930)

POCOCK, R.I.: 'Is the ferret a domesticated polecat?' (*The Field* 159, 1932)

RICE, R.P.: 'The Husbandry of Mink' (Proceedings of Symposium 5, The Association of British Wild Animal Keepers)

RYLAND, Lennox M.: 'Remission of estrus-associated anemia following ovariohysterectomy and multiple blood transfusions in a ferret' (*JAVMA*, Vol. 181, No. 8, 1982, pp. 820 ff)

RYLAND, L.M. and GORHAM, J.R.: 'The Ferret and its Diseases' (*JAVMA*, 173: 1154-8, 1978)

RYLAND, L.M., BERNARD, Susan L., GORHAM, John R.: 'A Clinical Guide to the Pet Ferret' (Vol. 5, No. 1, JU 83, Cont. Educn., Article No. 3)

TIMMINS, Nicholas: 'Ferrets who found the 'flu bug' (*The Times*, 30 May 1983)

WELCHMAN, D. de B., OXENHAM, M. and DONE, S.H.: 'Aleutian disease in domestic ferrets: diagnostic findings and survey results' (*Veterinary Record* (1993) 132, 479–484)

Surveillance (published by the New Zealand Ministry of Agriculture and Fisheries):

  Vol. 11, No. 2 1984 Special fitch issue

  Vol. 11, No. 1, Summer 1984:

    READ, D.H.: Survey of fitch for Aleutian disease virus and trace element status

    HUTTON, J.B.: Skin diseases (tail necrosis) in fitch

    SUTHERLAND, R.J. and RAMMELL, L.C.: Agalactia and fatty liver syndrome in nursing fitches

    READ, D.H.: Fitch kit deaths

    BROOKS, H.V.: Yellow fat disease (nutritional steatitis) in farmed fitch

    THORNTON, R.: Profile of ferret diseases encountered in 1983

    SUTHERLAND, R.J.: Posterior paralysis and lymphoplasmatic encephalomyelitis in fitch

    VICKERS, M.: Mycotic otitis and encephalitis in fitch

    THORNTON, R.: Non-suppurative meningo-encephalomyelitis in fitch

Vol. 10, No. 3:
  SUTHERLAND, R.J.: Mycotic otitis and meningo-encephalitis in the fitch
  FAIRLEY, R.: Pansteatitis in ferrets
  JAMES, M.P.: Zinc toxicity in fitch
Vol. 10, No. 2:
  COX, B.T.: Suspected Aleutian disease in fitch
  READ, D.H.: Mycotic otitis media and encephalitis in fitch
Vol. 10, No. 1:
  HORNER, G.W.: Plasmacytotis in a farmed fitch
Vol. 9, No. 3:
  Tuberculosis in fitches (Lincoln Animal Health Lab)
  Middle ear infection in ferrets (Invermay AHL)
Vol. 9, No. 2:
  Rickets in young ferrets (Lincoln AHL)
1976, No. 4:
  Swine 'flu in man there, cat 'flu in ferrets here
1974, No. 4:
  Mitey ferrets (Lincoln)

Index

(Page numbers in brackets indicate illustrations)